SPIRITUAL CARE

*Dietrich Bonhoeffer*_____

SPIRITUAL CARE

Translated and with an
Introduction by Jay C. Rochelle

FORTRESS PRESS

Translated from the German "*Seelsorge*," Band V, *Gesammelten Schriften* (Munich: Chr. Kaiser Verlag, 1982).

Biblical quotations, unless otherwise noted, are from the Revised Standard Version of the Bible, copyright 1946, 1952, © 1971, 1973 by the Division of Christian Education of the National Council of the Churches of Christ in the U.S.A. and are used by permission.

Library of Congress Cataloging in Publication Data

Bonhoeffer, Dietrich, 1906–1945.
  Spiritual care.
  "Translated from the German 'Seelsorge,' Band V,
Gesammelten Schriften (Munich: Chr. Kaiser Verlag,
1982)"—Verso t.p.
  Bibliography: p.
  1. Pastoral theology. 2. Clergy—Office. I. Title.
BV4010.B6313 1985   253   85–47711
ISBN 0–8006–1874–2

Printed in the United States of America   1-1874

16   17

Contents_____

Introduction

Finkenwalde was both a place and an idea. This small town in Pomerania, more associated in the minds of Germans of the 1930s with vacation than vocation, with pleasure than proclamation, became for a brief period the setting of one of the five preachers' seminaries of the Confessing church. It began 26 April 1935 in Zingst but was to start in earnest 24 June at Finkenwalde. Dietrich Bonhoeffer was called to be the principal of the seminary by Gerhard Jacobi, president of the Confessing church at Berlin.[1] Bonhoeffer disliked being called "principal" in public by the students, but he filled the position with characteristic vigor and singleness of purpose. This was to be, in Franz Hildebrandt's phrase, "the most fruitful period of his life."[2]

At Finkenwalde important things happened; here both *Cost of Discipleship* and *Life Together* were born, the latter most particularly from the experience of the gathered seminarians with their young principal (Bonhoeffer was not yet thirty years old when he was given this task by the Confessing church). The curriculum was developed with utmost care. The task of shaping each seminary was left to the individual principal, though ideas, problems, and programs were shared among them. Due to the clandestine nature of the operation, however, it was not possible for the administrative wing of the Confessing church to exercise much leadership; the principals had to be trusted.

Bonhoeffer's plan for the seminary involved the training of pastors as theologians, preachers, pastors, teachers, and administrators under the Word of God, persons who lived "as committed disciples."[3] This plan, which might in other circumstances have become a mere cliché, was the raison d'être for the existence of the seminary in Bonhoeffer's eyes. Unlike the traditional preachers' seminaries, in which only the practical aspects of ministry were taught in a technical-school setting, Bonhoeffer wrestled theologically with his students in order that they might confront the impact of the theology of the Word on pastoral work.

The governing concepts for Finkenwalde were those of Bonhoeffer's own life, and the call to serve as principal enabled the young theologian to affect directly the shaping of the ministry within the Confessing church. Bonhoeffer's theological work since the days of his doctoral thesis had focused on how Christ takes form in the world, which meant more narrowly a focus on ecclesiology. The christological lectures, delivered to an attentive crowd at the University of Berlin in 1933, marked a watershed of interpretation. Bonhoeffer had done a remarkable sociological study of the church for his doctoral dissertation (*The Communion of Saints*), in which he had put forth the church as a sociological category unique unto itself in that, unlike other human organizations, it was not a vehicle for some other goal but was, in fact, an end in itself, containing within its own proclamation and witness and work the very gifts it promises. Thus, within the church's proclamation and sacramental life, that grace which is eschatologically promised in the cross and resurrection of Jesus the Christ becomes present to the community and to the individual.

The Christology lectures (*Christ the Center*) reveal clearly the history of christological heresies as an aberration of the understanding not only of Jesus the Christ but of the church itself. Thus, the sociological study of the earlier years gives way to a theologically centered idea of church. But there is more.

Christ exists *for me*: this note of the reformer Luther was central to Bonhoeffer's own understanding of Christ in the Christology lectures. The purely academic approach is shunned in favor of an approach which embraces both scholarship and the existential question, Who is Christ for me?

This Christ *for me* must be available *to me* but not manipulable by me (otherwise the meaning of "Christ" is diminished). Bonhoeffer applies the dynamic idea of Word as event (*Geschehen*) to the figure of Christ as well; Christ comes to me in certain events, most specifically in Word and Sacrament and in the Christian community (*Gemeinde*). Christ becomes present in these forms in the same ambiguity as the historic Jesus; the congregation contains Christians who are both weak and strong because only in such a way can it be the body of Christ in the world, a body which is characterized by weakness as well as strength, by powerlessness as well as power, a body which is hidden in its disclosure and proclamation to the world as the *corpus Christi*.

Thus, it is not the presence of sinfulness in the congregation that is worthy of condemnation but, rather, the attempt to conceal sin. The church is the community of those who are forgiven and, because forgiven, are freed to live in service toward and intercession on behalf of others; this freedom is the concrete manifestation of the truth of resurrection in the life of the Christian. Christ takes form in the individual so that one becomes a "little Christ" to the neighbor (Luther, "Freedom of the Christian").

There is thus a direct connection between the revelation of God in Christ, the mediation of Christ to the community and its individual members, and the Christ-life which each Christian is called to live on behalf of the world. The key term in Bonhoeffer's writings which ties all of these three aspects of Christ together is *bearing*, and bearing is related to passion. Not without significance did one former student say of Bonhoeffer:

> To sit down at an instrument and improvise or even compose . . . can only be done in passion, and out of passion. Bonhoeffer cast this passion out of his life for the sake of a call to a greater "passion." This, too, is a contribution to the theme of "Call and Discipleship."[4]

Passion and bearing are related concepts, related in the person of Christ, related in the way one Christian bears another—about which Bonhoeffer wrote so passionately in *Life Together*.

One bears others because the Christian community is temporally imperfect, because it is weak, powerless, and hidden. We bear others because, like us, they come under the word of judgment and grace. Through the proclamation of Christ in our lives we become free to bear them and they to bear us—always recognizing that the greatest burden we must bear is that of another person's freedom.

There is an aristocracy of service in Bonhoeffer that demands our attention. This son of the upper middle class, raised in an actively intellectual and community-minded household, could not but choose a public life, despite the fact that it was a public life with which his siblings and father disagreed. By the same token, he could not but show a form of elitism, which is seen in his belief that even as the church is the elite manifestation of God's presence in the world, so there are elite within the church whose special calling it is to uphold the gospel in a clear and untainted way. This "elitism" is one of service and not domination, a possibility Bonhoeffer understood. The service takes place in various valid and divine estates. The collapse of the state was particularly poignant because it meant the reassessment of the nature of authentic Christian life in the world and spelled the end of a civil Christianity like that espoused in his boyhood home. It has, in fact, been thought that Bonhoeffer's protest against Nazism was initially based upon intense pain at the destruction of the grand order of Germany with its emphasis on honor, duty, and service.[5] It was the breakdown of a discipline that enabled freedom in service.[6]

The Christian pastor is the representative of Christ's authority in the congregation and, as such, will be the exemplar for bearing. One may see Bonhoeffer's lectures on spiritual care as an attempt to limn, through the traditional categories, the way in which a pastor may *bear* those in his or her care.

This bearing involves intercession: one must pray for those to whom one is committed. Such intercession is not to be taken lightly; more often than not, it will mean pain and suffering on the part of the one who prays. Since we are to be the form of Christ in the world, healing and reconciliation and also confrontation and disruption come through us in response to prayer; for we are meant, in the end, not only to pray but to be prayed through. The pastor is the one who must set this standard, and here is the spiritual elitism of which we earlier spoke.

The problem is that such elitism may be required of those who are not ready to render it as their proper service. Thus, the pastorate is stressed as office rather than as charism. We do not rely on gifts. The pastorate is not a kind of shamanism but a peculiar form of priesthood. Thus, we must understand the tools the church has provided as the proper channels by which spiritual care takes place. The church must not be left to the rule of the guru or spiritually adept; the cultural values of honor, duty, and office certainly apply within the church as in all of society. Through the discipline of spiritual care as outlined in these lectures, Bonhoeffer aimed to offer a form for being and acting in the pastorate which would ensure that the contingencies would be arranged for the recognition of the Christ who exists as Word, Sacrament, and community. This service was thus a proclamation central to the functioning of the pastor because in these forms Christ comes to community and to individual, the former through the Word and Sacraments in public worship, the latter through spiritual care. One's life leads, according to Bonhoeffer's poem, from discipline to action to suffering to freedom. If there is an elitism here, it is in our calling to enter the fray and to care, to suffer (same Latin root as for "bearing").[7]

The Christ who bears the sin of the world becomes present in church (the term is *Gemeinde,* which can also be translated as "congregation," and it is usually clear that he means both a theological and social description by this term; in any case, he means more than a building or an aggregate of people). *Christus als Gemeinde existierend* is a characteristic phrase: "Christ *exists* as the community/congregation."

Christ may be an idea we have about God, or Christ may become an address in which we are confronted by God. In order for a personal relationship to occur, the latter is essential. An idea does not compel us to make decisions, and it is clear from the witness of the Bible and the church throughout history that nothing occurs in the relationship between Christ and believer apart from decision: we are called in Jesus of Nazareth by an address, and we must decide whether that address comes from God or from insanity.[8] It is always a risk to make a decision either way. Christ will not let us go once we have made the decision to "follow"; there is a compelling presence in the biblical and ecclesial witness to Christ which will not let us go. In the end we know that the witness and the Christ are one and the same. The fact that the church is called "body of Christ" and the sacrament of the altar is called "body of Christ" and that we are individually members of that "body of Christ" is but one fact expressed in three different ways.

If we follow this line of reasoning as we consider the *Spiritual Care,* we see that the main end of the process is to enable a meeting between Christ and the person to take place; to that end, all obstacles are to be removed. One might go so far as to say that the only purpose of spiritual care is to enable this life-giving meeting to occur; then, one steps aside gracefully to allow the conversation to go on. For this reason, Bonhoeffer begins by telling us that spiritual care is a function of the congregation and that it is an aspect of the broader, more encompassing activity of *proclamation.*

It is the nature of God, according to Christian faith, to compri lectical aspects. These dialectical aspects have been expressed by ber of concepts: law and gospel, hidden and revealed, judg deemer (and sanctifier). The reality of God is known in encounters where both aspects of God are simultaneously known by the person. Rudolf Otto's masterwork, *The Idea of the Holy*, presented us with this dialectical understanding of God from the liturgical perspective; Barth's work is always written on the razor edge of the dialectic.

Bonhoeffer was aware that the Lutheran sin was to neglect the comprehended dualities in the nature of God by disregarding one aspect at the expense of the other. In *Cost of Discipleship*, he identified this sin in his notion of "cheap grace," that grace which justifies the sin without the justification of the sinner. This form of "grace" rests in the failure to see that a genuine encounter with God invariably involves judgment as well. Otto's idea of the *mysterium tremendum et fascinosum* serves this understanding well; God is the One who embraces both attraction, mysterious, fascinating, and awesome, and a form of repulsion that is grounded in the absolute otherness, the holiness of God that is terrible. The proclamation of God to humanity requires, at all times, both aspects. To cut the dialectic leads, in the case of law, to a God who is pure wrath and judgment and, in the case of gospel, to a God who is pure grace and into whom we disappear as into a warm bath. In the former case, God's immanence is destroyed by God's transcendence; in the latter, the transcendence is swallowed up in immanence.

Thus, the hidden and revealed, judging and gracing God comes to us in the person and work of Jesus Christ, and this Christ is now known among us through and as Word, Sacrament, and community. Christ always comes to us as concrete address. Spiritual care is one form in which Christ becomes present. As Clifford Green writes:

> Christ is present in the form of human speech, acts, and relationships in the Word and sacraments of the Gemeinde; Christ's mediatorial function is interpreted in relation to the anthropological categories of man's history, his being as and in nature, and his sociality. . . . Bonhoeffer's innovation derived from his thinking in terms of sociality: he makes the personal relations of preacher and addressed in the community *intrinsic* to the nature of the Word as the *personal* presence of Christ. The other man who is *extra me* is the form of Christ as Other who is *pro me*; the Word is *essentially social*, and cannot be separated from this relationship and encounter of persons.[9]

Christ doesn't exist in isolation; either the Word becomes flesh and a fully incarnational theology becomes possible, or the Word remains outside human experience entirely and ends without power. The historic Lutheran position has been the former, and it has been known in a formula, *finitum capax infiniti*: the finite is capable of bearing the infinite—though this is miracle and not the normal or the expected.[10] Spiritual care is one form of the incarnation of the Word in the midst of the congregation. Bonhoeffer's critique of psychotherapy as he knew it might begin at this point. Psychotherapy, in his understanding, did not leave the person to him or herself but came as a form of bonding which became bondage—which would be the opposite of an incarnation *pro me*, which completes me by making me more fully myself, yet "in Christ."

Thus, the confessional experience, that format in which we confess our sin before another and receive the assurance of forgiveness, is central to the proclamation of the gospel and therefore central to the work of spiritual care. Spiritual care is nothing other than a personalizing of the proclamation which—of necessity, due to the shape of public worship—is made in a general way in the congregation. Spiritual care leads from and returns to the content of the proclamation, which is God active in Christ to bring new life out of sin and death. We are personally brought into the sphere where this word of resurrection can claim and restore us to life.

In *Spiritual Care*, Bonhoeffer deals with ultimates. The whole text demands us to consider how the gospel message is brought to people in the midst of their personal lives, and his message and counsel use the tools given within the traditional life of the church. Baptism, wedding, funeral, and pastoral visitation are the spokes radiating from a center rooted in confession and forgiveness.

The Text Bonhoeffer's understanding of spiritual care is rooted in two theological principles. On one hand, there is the Word of God with its double function of law and gospel. This is the formal, dynamic center of spiritual care, and everything revolves around it.

On the other hand is the commission to proclaim the Word. The Word is always the word of address, the word of proclamation. There is no room in Bonhoeffer's understanding of spiritual care for personal aggrandizement or affect. Spiritual care is part of the call of the gospel, and Bonhoeffer opposes any sort of "spiritual direction" which may be based upon spiritual authority or superiority, in which one partner of the conversation is subjected to the other. Both partners stand beneath and within the dynamic presence of God announced and occasioned by the Word; both partners are addressed by the same law and freed by the same gospel. Spiritual care (in a way similar to baptism) is a personal address of that Word which is the treasure and the authentic mark of the whole church. In *Spiritual Care*, we are confronted with the awesome truth that in speech God's presence is known and that speech is also our own; in silence God's presence is known and that silence is also our own.

But there are no immediate relationships in the Christian community, and that belief is underwritten in *Spiritual Care* (later this concept comes to full bloom in the text of *Life Together*). There can be no immediacy of relationships within the church, for the church is the body of Christ, and thus Christ, as its head, governs all those relationships within the church. Christ is the mediator not only between God and humanity but between persons within the church. We meet in and only in Christ, which makes the emphasis on the equality of address essential to the practice of spiritual care. The church is not an assembly of like-minded individuals, nor is it an agency organized around certain previously agreed-upon principles (like a social agency or a labor union). The church is entered through baptism, and it is baptism which gives us our relationship within the church. We are tied together in the body of Christ even if we don't like each other. Community is not the same thing as camaraderie.

Bonhoeffer makes a distinction between personality and *Amt*. The *Amt* (office) within the church is more important than the personality. It is not the personality of the pastor that is essential to spiritual care but the call of the gospel to the office of proclamation. Bonhoeffer understands the call to be reciprocal; that is, if the pastor will not function properly, it is the task of the congregation to hold the pastor in love in such a way that the functions begin to be carried out. One might call this accountability, but that is a term Bonhoeffer did not use even if the concept seems to be at work. There must be signals from the pastor to the congregation of a willingness to function as a curate of souls. The lecture notes show Bonhoeffer's willingness to risk the judgment of scrupulosity so that no offense should be given that would detract from the pastoral office. The point is clear, however: the objectivity of the Word must be maintained at all costs. Religion and Christianity must, in accord with the theology of the Word, be separated; no one may be allowed to reduce the gospel to the level of feelings or interpersonal relationships.

There is, however, an inconsistency in the text which is not solved. Only hints of a solution appear in the final writings that we possess in English as *Letters and Papers from Prison* and *Fiction from Prison*. In these writings, Bonhoeffer is finally willing to disclose his own struggles in the faith, his personal thoughts and doubts, his joys and sorrows. But in *Spiritual Care*, we find a Bonhoeffer removed from the text, a person who stands aloof from the text in much the same way he would have us separate religion from Christianity. Only the latter is of importance, so for Bonhoeffer a personal approach would have ruined the message he had to proclaim. He must stand aside, and he advises a style of ministry in which one stands aside and uses the tools provided by the church's tradition, almost in an uncritical fashion, to communicate Christ to others.[11]

The inconsistency, unrelieved in the text, is between a style of behavior that calls for a kind of spiritual elitism, a moral superiority, on one hand, and on the other, an official ministry in which such matters are of no moment whatsoever (in fact, they cannot be admitted into the discussion without ruining the objectivity of the proclamation). One must live a circumspect life, but this does not figure into any spiritual conversations; in that arena, only the Word is to hold sway.

This dialectic is that of Bonhoeffer's own life, for the struggle within him was between hero and servant, and he had grown up in the age of the "great man" theory of history. To the great man Hitler, there needed to be opposed another great man for the battle to be won. The ambiguity is between the forms of greatness; "Among you, whoever would be greatest must be the servant of all" (Mark 10:45 and parallels).

Bonhoeffer emphasizes love in *Spiritual Care*, and the emphasis is a welcome one. He knows the possibility of choosing favorites in a parish setting, the possibility of tendentiousness, and the trials faced by team ministries when parishioners deal unevenly with their pastors or try to get one to side with them against the other. His wise counsel is that one must live by the principle of *agape*, which sets for us a higher goal than the development of interpersonal relations (while not denying the need for them; he has suggestions in the area of friendship). The principle of *agape* frees us from partiality.

The operative center for spiritual care is individual confession and forgiveness. All conversation in spiritual care revolves around this center.

Pastoral conversation has precise boundaries and a precise content. It is spiritual care in the verbal mode. Such conversation proceeds from the call to proclaim law and gospel and does not overstep that boundary. Spiritual care is, above all, not "advice" or "help"—any such conception would be detrimental to the office. The Word is addressed in its fullness to an individual whose position in the life of faith is taken seriously. Much of the text deals with spiritual care to the uncommitted, the educated, the sick, and the dying.

The conversation aims toward the development, creation, and edification of the body of Christ and of the individual member of the body. The body of Christ is created through forgiveness, a note later struck decisively in *Life Together* that had been sounded in austere ways in *Cost of Discipleship*. In *Spiritual Care*, Bonhoeffer is moving from the austerity of grace into a consideration of how such grace becomes enacted, enfleshed, incarnate in the Christian community.

It comes, in the end, to the forgiveness of sins. There is no other name for that word which comes from "outside" to a person in existential doubt and despair, to one who has known the woe of estrangement and the deep, shattering chaos of alienation, that peculiar sense of floating without order or anchor or symbolic handhold in a world which has gone blank of meaning and faintly—if not wholly—hostile of purpose.

Such a word is more than markings on paper; it is proclamation in that it has objectivity; it is address in that it claims us in our subjectivity; it is release in that it uncouples us from guilt and frees us for responsibility; it is act in that it comes not mentally but also physically, bodily enacted, in ritual cycles. An action is something which intervenes in the natural course of life, which is intentional in that intervention, and which has consequences both known and unknown. The proclamation of forgiveness is such an act. Such a word brings new life and future to those who, hearing it aright (that is to say, hearing it within and understanding it to be a true and wholesome word addressed to them as entire persons) act on it, live with it, play with it, and stand on it as the grounds for a more meaningful presence in the world.

The word of forgiveness comes to those who live life to the fullest and deepest, who engage in struggle at the extremes. Those who hate and those who love, those who desire order and those who live with chaos, those who weep and those who rejoice, those who celebrate and those who refuse to celebrate: these are some who are ready for the life in God proffered by forgiveness.

Only to those who have known the grievous power of sin will the proclamation of forgiveness come as good news; the dead are those in need of the proclamation of resurrection. The church is not for those who feel themselves to be whole so much as it is for those who, having gone as far as they can under their own power, are prepared to risk the faith that there is a power beyond them in which they are personally fulfilled. The church is for those whose yearnings for self-transcendence and transformation crack on the knowledge that we who would transform ourselves are imperfect tools for the job and that we do not really know what we would like to become. The idea that we must transform ourselves always disappears when we consider who it is that is supposed to do the transforming. Evangelical Christianity is not interested in self-transformation but, rather, in the donation of new life.

Forgiveness implies a declaration of our value, dignity, and worth that is beyond the vicissitudes of feeling, although it comes to us at the core of our subjectivity. Forgiveness offers us the actuality of new life through Christ. Forgiveness is a declaration event by which the barrier between the human and a saving knowledge of God is broken. Christ is the actor in whom this barrier is broken, and most specifically is he that actor in cross and resurrection.

Intercessory prayer plays a major role in spiritual care. The pastor is intercessor who bears the trials of those known from congregation and community and world; from this bearing comes the knowledge of how to speak the word to an individual Christian. Bonhoeffer later expanded the role of intercessor to a full chapter in *Life Together*, entitled "The Ministry of Bearing."

Conversations that are part of spiritual care point to the Word and Sacrament as the healing gifts of a gracious God. Bonhoeffer abjures the use of psychoanalytic methods because they rest on a different footing, anthropologically and philosophically, from the traditional cure of souls upon which he builds his models. Spiritual care, for him, involves no stock in a "method" as one might find in various therapies and psychoanalytical schools. He is critically aware of the doctor/patient model in analysis and goes so far as to call it "bondage" because it rests on a false distinction between persons that cannot be maintained under a theology of Word and cross.

The text comes from a world in rapid disintegration. He is aware of and attacks the Nazi regime in this text in a most unusual way; his objection is based on the interference of the state in the keeping of the Fourth Commandment. This is the only direct reference to the state in the lectures. The lectures come from a world in which absolutes were still discernible and believed; relationships and roles were ordered and played a more significant part in human society than in the egalitarian United States of our time.

We no longer live in such a world, and neither did Bonhoeffer by the end of his life, less than ten years after the beginning of his lectures on spiritual care at Finkenwalde. The central argument remains clear and useful to us, but there are no longer the structures by which the total text might become applicable, even if we wished to make it so. Although Bonhoeffer knows well the distinction between office and personality, the world in which we live has by and large chosen the latter over the former and, in so doing, has not only made the exercise of office far more difficult but has opened up the question of authority in church and state in ways Bonhoeffer would not and could not have done.

The issue of responsibility is not dealt with in the text. We have come to use terms like accountability and mutual responsibility in ways Bonhoeffer did not and, perhaps, would not do. This accounts, in part, for the extensive place the *role* of curate of souls occupies, while no hints are given as to where the pastor's responsibility ends and that of the parishioner begins. This is a problem that receives consideration only at the very end of Bonhoeffer's life (see the essay by Ruth Zerner in *Fiction from Prison*).[12] Thus, we are left with the inconsistency mentioned above between the life style of the pastor and the theological principle of equality under the address of law and gospel. There is hope, nevertheless, that an emphasis on an educational model that emphasizes church as community, and as place of confession and forgiveness, would give birth to a style of spiritual care such as Bonhoeffer envisions—a spiritual care rooted in the God who promises to be present in Word and sacraments, a spiritual care which draws its life-giving water from the images, texts, dramas, and symbols of the liturgical and ritual cycle of the community.

The Antecedents In the early Christian centuries, no distinction existed between the four theological disciplines; these names—the historic, systematic, biblical, and practical—date from the time of Schleiermacher, who regarded *Seelsorge* as of major importance, the means whereby the individual gains identity.[13] Theology was not divided between philosophy and contemplation. The aim of theology was to lead to doxology; theology was rooted in liturgy, Bible, and prayer rather than in logic. The aim of the theologian was wonder and worship, and one can make a splendid case for the doxological basis of both creed and doctrine in the early church.[14] Practical theology and other forms of theology were of a piece; the cure of souls was connected primarily to the moral and ritual life of the church: preparation for baptism and eucharist and attention to ongoing ethical problems formed the basis for the practice.[15]

Although one finds a comprehension of the spiritual life and of the priesthood in John Chrysostom's six books *On the Priesthood,*[16] the whole is characterized by an extreme moral asceticism. This was apparently a protest against the characteristic lack of integrity in the age. Thus, his is an abortive attempt, marred by excesses of misogynism and an almost Manichean, puritanical streak.

With Gregory the Great, we find the genuine beginnings of an emphasis on pastoral care—subsumed under the rubric of servitude as a mode of spirituality. The emphasis is on the doing of one's duty in service to humanity; insofar as this is concerned with life in the priesthood, pastoral care becomes the vehicle for expressions of service.[17]

From the Celtic church, where priests were sparse and roads and other links of communication difficult and in many places nonexistent between towns, there grew up the practice of the *anmchara,* or soul friend, who was a layperson.[18] In the Irish church in particular, the emphasis on confession was heavy, and an elaborate system of penitential practice grew. Confessors were lay people, and absolution was understood to be given in the celebration when one attended mass.[19] The practice of individual confession entered the Roman church through the Celtic church until "penance" (the medieval name for the ritual) became a regular feature of western Christianity. Priestly absolution came in the twelfth century.

The spiritual director is a figure who emerges from a number of different locales. One could trace spiritual direction back to the desert fathers, the eremitical monks of the Egyptian desert in the fourth century C.E. who received visitors and offered spiritual guidance.[20] From them

the figure of the *staretz*, very familiar in the Russian church, is ultimately derived: the *staretz* is a "fool for Christ," who functions as a spiritual director to numbers of people who attach themselves to him.[21] In
the western church the Dominicans were influential in the Middle Ages
and early modern period for their work in spiritual direction.

In the high Middle Ages, the notion of spiritual friendship was carefully developed by Aelred, abbot of the monastery at Rievaulx (in what
is today Yorkshire in England). In many ways, his work is an anticipa-
tion of that work which would be done later by the friars of the Domin-
ican Order. Aelred's work rests on Cicero's *de Amicitiae*, with important
additions (most notably the Christocentricity of the relationship and
the emphasis on intercessory prayer—both of which are to be found
nine centuries later in the writings of Bonhoeffer, especially in *Spiritual
Care* and in *Life Together*).[22]

A final tributary that leads into the evangelical concept of spiritual
care is, of course, to be found in the work of the reformer Luther,
whose own method involved the keeping of a large correspondence as
part of his spiritual care. These "letters of spiritual counsel" contain interesting historical insights into the meaning of pastoral care in the Reformation period.[23]

We should begin, however, by looking at Luther's approach to confession and forgiveness. Briefly put, Luther altered the medieval understanding of the sacrament of "penance" in several ways:

1. He dropped the notion that there should be an elaborate enumeration of sins in the confessional act; the penitent was not encouraged to
dredge up all the sins he or she had committed. Only those which
"troubled the conscience" were to be confessed;

2. No "penance" was to be assessed; in opposition to the medieval
practice by which one was given a token amendment to perform,
Luther dropped such a token;

3. In connection with the above, he placed the stress on the proclamation of forgiveness itself, since this is the real gift in the practice; it is
the gospel, and nothing should be allowed to detract from it.

Luther was concerned that confession should not be exhaustive and
thus focus attention more on the penitent than on the gracious Word of
God which was offered in God's stead by the pastor. Also, he was concerned that confession should not be mechanical. Though Luther called
for and supported the retention of individual confession and forgive-

ness in the total life of the church and wished to see it used more than the perfunctory once a year, he felt that it should be voluntary.

Thus, Luther both simplified the ritual and at the same time sought to emphasize that which he considered of major importance in the whole interchange—namely, the address of the penitent with the sure word of forgiveness.[24] This surety is seen, for example, in the *Lutheran Book of Worship*'s order for individual confession and forgiveness, where the pastor asks the penitent: "Do you believe that the forgiveness I am about to declare comes from God?" To which the penitent responds, "Yes," following which there is a declaration of forgiveness in Trinitarian language accompanied by the laying-on of hands and completed by the sharing of the peace.[25]

Spiritual care in Luther builds upon this foundation of forgiveness; it is aimed at the "distressed and sick soul" and thus is concerned with the whole person before God rather than before other persons.

Luther's spiritual father, Johannes Staupitz, had once told him, "Why do you torment yourself with speculations? Took instead at the wounds of Christ and at his blood shed for you, from these predestination will shine forth." He also advised Luther to read the Scriptures, so that in them he would find life abundant. Thus, Luther's was to be a practical rather than a speculative spirituality, a spirituality which was concerned with the proclamation and the hearing of the Word; for in the Word, God's presence was to be found. This practical spirituality became functional in a style of spiritual care.

With the sick, Luther's basic approach was to visit, to inquire after the nature of the illness, to ask how the person was coming along and how patient he or she was in the presence of pain and/or illness. Luther counseled the sick that whether we live or die, we are in God's hands because of the sacrifice of Christ. Luther counseled the welcoming of death by all persons because it represented the onset of a fuller life with God; even if the patient recovered, this was to be viewed as a reprieve of the inevitable, and one should not forget the end of life. This was, however, not a counsel of despair or morbidity; Luther's was a rich and robust life, and his counsel was meant to remind people of the constant presence of God in their lives—whether they lived or died, they were in the Lord.

In dealing with those who were errant, Luther always pointed to Christ as the mediator between God and humanity and to the Word as central to our self-understanding as well as to our understanding of God. He often suggested, in accord with Staupitz's suggestion, to stay with the revealed Word of God and not to ask after what is not revealed.[26]

A letter to Albrecht, Graf Mansfeld, from 28 December 1542, contains the following interesting note about intercessory prayer as viewed by Luther: "I am concerned for the soul of your reverend grace, which I cannot bear to have cast out of my care and prayers, for that would to me mean—just as truly—cast out of the church."[27] Here is a serious concern with and conception of the body of Christ that is characteristic of much thinking among Lutherans and that is evident in Bonhoeffer's *Spiritual Care*.

In dealing with those who mourned, Luther exhorted people to exorcise the spirit of sadness and to draw comfort from the Word, with its promise of salvation and life through the cross and resurrection of Christ. He was quite faithful in writing to the bereaved in his care, and he points to two sources of comfort; first, that those who have died have died in faith; and second, that the will of God is for the best, even if it involves pain and sorrow, for this will is preeminently known in the cross of Christ which is a sign for all the suffering we know in our lives. Grief is necessary and a normal, healthy, and natural part of human life, but it must not become extreme; one must not dote on it. In his letters, Luther often used biblical portraits as examples of empathic experience from which the bereaved may take comfort.

For those who were depressed and vexed by temptation, Luther had three basic counsels:

1. Take comfort in the Word. The Word of God is needed in your fight against the evil one; you cannot fight this battle on your own. It is unevenly matched. Christ in the wilderness of temptation had to rely upon the Word of God even though he was the Word of God incarnate; how much more, then, must we rely upon the Word to enable us to overcome temptation and despair;

2. Continue with your life as normally as you can; eat and drink, and do not deny yourself the regular necessities of life. Luther knew that lonely people tend not to care for the body. He suggested that solitude is only for the strong in faith; all others need company and normalcy;

3. Involve yourself with the companionship and conversation of Christian friends; take their counsel to be the Word of God for you in the midst of your despair.

Luther counseled that external temptations are easier to deal with than those which he called *Anfechtungen* (an existential temptation); resistance was essential to the process. One must take comfort in the temptations of Christ; they are useful to strengthen and to teach us in the midst of our own temptations. Music and laughter are good antidotes: "One has to laugh and joke a little . . . ," Luther wrote to Jerome Weller on 6 November 1530; the devil is to be laughed at.[28]

It can be seen from this brief overview that many of the classic approaches in spiritual care have been in existence since the time of the Reformation, if not before. *Spiritual Care* stands in a long tradition in the Lutheran church, a tradition seen in older manuals of pastoral care.[29] In the last forty years, however, pastoral care has been dominated by psychological methods and language while this older model has been relegated to the background.[30] This book is a small attempt at re-examination of an older tradition.

The Word of God The task of pastoral ministry is, above all else, to arrange the contingencies for an encounter with the Divine. The pastor is one who authorizes, authenticates, and supports the search for God (who is always present and therefore not "lost" except in the lives of those who are dulled or immured to the presence) in the light of contemporary needs.

This means, in the evangelical tradition, that the pastor begins by announcing that the search for God has been ended — in the Word which was effective in creation, now become incarnate in Jesus the Christ, and which lives as voice within the church in proclamation and sacraments.

The use of Word and Sacrament in spiritual care is a derivation from their use in the believing community; such use is a personal form of address, a personal application of the means of grace by which the whole church is edified and strengthened. Two things need be noted. First, spiritual care in this sense is for those of the household of faith. The process differs not only from psychological counseling but also from pastoral counseling centers that function as a community service. Second, the pastoral act of spiritual care is not an end in itself; it is aimed at freeing persons for service to God and world through their apprehension of the many dimensions of faith. It is aimed toward faith active in love.

Since it is not possible from the biblical perspective for human beings to live whole lives apart from the rest of humanity (let alone apart from a relatedness to God), an approach to spiritual care that is individualistic is automatically distorted and may become unfaithful to the biblical witness and to the church. Christianity offers no place to "do your own thing." The aim of spiritual care is the integration of the person with the human community, beginning with one's relationship to God in the community of faith.

There are correct and incorrect forms for the democratization of faith in evangelical perspective. Spiritual care is sometimes seen as a form of spiritual elitism. At bottom, this objection is related to an incorrect notion of faith's democratization—namely, that no one can assist another person toward the realization and flowering of faith. The fear is that the world will break down into gurus and their followers. However, the insistence on such individualism also led to the horrors of the myth of "private interpretation" of the Scriptures, which produced many splinter groups in Christianity founded on idiosyncratic understandings of the Bible and such clear divergencies from the historic catholic faith as Christian Science and the Jehovah's Witnesses.

A true democratization of faith, however, which is represented in the Reformation teaching of the universal priesthood of believers, is rooted in the primacy of the Word, from which flows the priesthood. In the universal priesthood, one functions as a "priest" for another person in three ways: first, by praying for the person—intercession is the major form of priesthood and is the spiritual form of mediation and offering on behalf of others; second, by teaching in whatever ways one can—in our time this means the sharing of Christian stories with one another and the mutual exploration of the meaning of faith; and third, by that process known as the "mutual exhortation and consolation among Christians"—a way of being with others which begins from the assumption of a shared network of images, stories, and rituals, especially the shared entry into the faith through baptism, the common sacrament which unites us all in Christ and with one another in the church.

Spiritual care is a process in which both participants enact their roles as members of the universal priesthood, in which both stand under the word of judgment and grace, and in which all counsel is judged by and emanates from the body of catholic faith, which is a believed faith before it is a faith in which one believes. We inherit a tradition with which we must come to terms; we do not invent the faith or the sacraments out of whole cloth. The faith of the church precedes our individual faith and acts as check and monitor on our personal faith.

The pastor as curate of souls and the layperson who functions as curate of souls, under the impetus of a gift in that direction and a calling to service, do not possess magic or secret knowledge but are able to communicate the depth of faith into the life of another person. Spiritual care thus proceeds from the evangelical emphasis on Word and Sacrament as the creative power for the community of faith (Augsburg Confession, article VII).

The concept *vocation* assumes there is One who calls me, One who stands over against me as well as with me, One who is different from me as well as the ground of my own being and becoming; this One is an Other whom I would not know apart from being called. Vocation, apart from its further meaning in the Lutheran tradition, stands against all notions of religion composed of rummaging about on the inside of a person for new spiritual frontiers. Vocation is a barrier against all forms of spirituality which are but pathways to self-transcendence. What is called into existence is not merely what would have been found in ourselves in any case, given enough time and insight, but the new humanity in Christ. This means that, if the curate of souls substitutes personal, religious insight for the proclamation of God, "thus is the cure of souls debased into its caricature, the sedation of souls."[31] We have no general religious word to bring to another person. Vocation only makes sense as God enters time and space; if God is pure transcendence, any notion of a call from God within the structures of our life or, more, of our calling upon God, is meaningless. The traditional teaching of *kenosis*, the humiliation of God in Christ, tries to safeguard the paradoxical presence of the One who is revealed yet still hidden in the figure of Jesus. Christianity, as the incarnation of God, has no impulse to move people beyond the material realm into a supposed realm of pure spirit; such a movement contradicts the very foundation of the faith. Spiritual care begins with the call of Jesus to "follow me" and moves from there into the world, not away from it, but a world which is perceived differently because of the presence of God in it; one sees the world *sub specie aeternitatis*, "from the viewpoint of eternity," because of undergoing that radical change of mind called *metanoia*. Henceforth, all of life is penetrated with the fragile, hidden, yet resplendent presence of the Divine and the spiritual in the midst of the common and the material.

Spiritual care involves invocation—a calling into our presence of the One who calls us into being. We cannot forget the audacity of invoking God's presence. That the finite world bears the infinite God is an insight of endless meaning for meditation and prayer. If we lose our knowledge that invocation is gift and miracle, we enter a path which inexorably leads us to callousness and to what Bonhoeffer called "cheap grace," in which transcendence is naturally swallowed up by immanence (and from our viewpoint, God is taken for granted).[32]

The other form of invocation in spiritual care is intercession—the invoking of God's healing presence in the lives of others.

Revocation is the complement of invocation. This is First Commandment business; it is the exposure and exorcism of the demons and idols by which we construct false selves apart from the sustaining Word of God. It is the peeling away of those penultimates by which we deflect the ultimate call of God in our lives, beginning with those images of God we hold which must be broken.[33]

Evocation is the main form of spiritual care; this is an alternate term by which to speak of that conversation which is aimed at the awareness of God's presence in a person's life. Spiritual care evokes the soul (*Seelsorge* is the *Sorge*—which word bears the double entendre of caring and sorrow or pathos—for the *Seele*), that self which is gift and creation of God and not the constructed ego; spiritual care reaches below the surface for the person who is named by the Word.

Under the rubric of evocation, personal experience may be examined. It may sound up to this point as if spiritual care is austere in insisting on examining the history of faith in a person's life apart from the examination of worship and personal experience. But these have their place: worship is the locus where the images and stories and the tradition we carry within us are born. It is said by the sages that Abram came to faith through the contemplation of nature; this legend is meant to tell us that the God of nature is the God of history, in the end, and that we need not fear that the God whom we conceive in personal insight is ultimately the God disclosed in revelation. The task of the curate of souls is not to reject personal experience but to assist people in incorporating their experience within the dimensions of the catholic faith. Spiritual care is invitational; it is not prescriptive. It is anchored in discoveries which are evoked, rather than in doctrines which are imposed. Though the curate of souls must be anchored in the living catholic tradition, the primary material with which one works is always the living call that is heard, accepted, followed, and resisted in the individual's life.

In sum, in spiritual care we explore how people have been called by God, what they are called to be and to do in response to that call and in the light of their baptism. The dimension of forgiveness which is at the center of the enterprise of spiritual care offers a release from false callings, "from the danger of being trapped in lofts without light, without motion."[34] The Eucharist offers a communal context for exploring the call in all of life. The mutual exhortation and consolation of the faithful offer a model of disclosure and discovery for the depth of Jesus' call to "follow me."

In the end, there is nothing to "believe" in a static sense; there is no final statement of a doctrinal position or tenet that one can cling to throughout life as a conceptual truth. The truth of Christianity is only known relationally, and the origin of the relation is the Word, the living presence of God in Christ known in action and image and drama and speech and silence within the Christian community, especially in the action-speech of baptism and Eucharist and prayer. One can only live in the present moment attuned to the Word, in the knowledge that it is the Word which holds one in existence and offers one the grace both of sustenance and of authentic identity. The Word is so close to us that we cannot insert a piece of paper between the self and the creative Word of God; it is the task of spiritual care to enable people to become alive to this Word at their center.

2 TIM 1:8-10

NOTES

1. Cf. "Drawn to Suffering," in *I Knew Dietrich Bonhoeffer*, eds. Wolf-Dieter Zimmerman and R. Gregor Smith, trans. Kaethe Gregor Smith (New York and Evanston: Harper & Row, 1966), 71–74.

2. Cf. Franz Hildebrandt, "An Oasis of Freedom," in *I Knew Bonhoeffer*, 40.

3. Cf. Paul Lehmann, "The Paradox of Discipleship," in *I Knew Bonhoeffer*, 41–45.

4. Cf. Johannes Goebel, in *I Knew Bonhoeffer*, 124.

5. Cf. Otto Dudzus, "Arresting the Wheel," in *I Knew Bonhoeffer*, 82; also Dietrich Bonhoeffer, *Letters and Papers from Prison*, enl. edition, ed. and trans. Eberhard Bethge (New York: Macmillan Co., 1972), 294, and Bonhoeffer, *Fiction from Prison*, English edition ed. Renate and Eberhard Bethge with Clifford Green, trans. Ursula Hoffman (Philadelphia: Fortress Press, 1981), 141–43, 153.

6. Cf. Hellmut Traub, "Two Recollections," in *I Knew Bonhoeffer*, 159–61.

7. Cf. Bonhoeffer, *Gesammelte Schriften*, ed. Eberhard Bethge (Munich: Chr. Kaiser Verlag, 1958–61), 3:193.

8. Cf. Clifford Green, *Bonhoeffer: The Sociality of Christ and Humanity* (Missoula, Mont.: Scholars Press, 1972), 255–57.

9. Ibid., 276.

10. Cf. my article, "What Price *Finitum Capax Infiniti*," *Academy* 38, nos. 3, 4 (1982): 110–21; also Carl E. Braaten, *Principles of Lutheran Theology* (Philadelphia: Fortress Press, 1983).

11. One might contend that this is due to the construction of the text of *Spiritual Care*, since it is a compilation of notes, but the phenomenon shows up in much of the corpus.

12. Cf. Ruth Zerner, "Dietrich Bonhoeffer's Prison Fiction," in *Fiction from Prison*, 139–67.

13. Cf. Edward Farley, *Theologia* (Philadelphia: Fortress Press, 1983).

14. Cf. among others the standard resources by J. N. D. Kelly, *Early Christian Creeds* (New York: Longman, Inc., 1981), and *Early Christian Doctrines* (New York: Harper & Row, 1981); and see Robert Jenson, *The Triune Identity* (Philadelphia: Fortress Press, 1982).

15. Cf. Josef Jungmann, *Pastoral Liturgy* (Notre Dame, Ind.: Univ. of Notre Dame Press, 1957); Marion Hatchett, *Sanctifying Life, Time, and Space* (New York: Seabury Press, 1976).

16. Cf. John Chrysostom, *On the Priesthood*, trans. and intr. Graham Neville (Crestwood, N.Y.: SVS Press, 1977).

17. Gregory the Great, *Pastoral Care*, trans. Henry Davis; Ancient Christian Writers Series 11 (Westminster, Md.: Newman Press, 1950); for full commentary on Gregory's approach to pastoral care, cf. Thomas C. Oden, *Care of Souls in the Classic Tradition* (Philadelphia: Fortress Press, 1984).

18. Works in this field are burgeoning, but three major ones to consult are: Tilden Edwards, *Spiritual Friend* (New York: Paulist Press, 1980); Urban T. Holmes, *Spirituality for Ministry* (New York: Harper & Row, 1982); and Kenneth Leech, *Soul Friend* (New York: Harper & Row, 1980).

19. John T. McNeill and Helena M. Gamer, *Medieval Handbooks of Penitence* (New York: Octagon Books, 1965).

20. Sr. Benedicta Ward, *The Wisdom of the Desert Fathers*, intr. Archbishop Anthony Bloom (Oxford, England: SVG Press, 1975); Thomas Merton, *The Wisdom of the Desert* (New York: New Dimensions, 1960).

21. Cf. Archimandrite Sophrony, *Wisdom from Mount Athos*, trans. Rosemary Edmonds (Crestwood, N.Y.: SVS Press, 1974).

22. Cf. Aelred of Rievaulx, *Spiritual Friendship*, trans. Mary Eugenia Laker SSND, intr. Douglass Roby (Kalamazoo, Mich.: Cistercian Publications, no. 5, 1977).

23. Cf. August F. Nebe, *Luther as Spiritual Advisor* (Philadelphia: Lutheran Publication House, 1894); Theodore Tappert, *Luther's Letters of Spiritual Counsel*, Westminster Library of Christian Classics, vol. 10 (Philadelphia: Westminster Press, 1957).

24. Cf. American edition, Vol. 35, 3-22, "The Sacrament of Penance, 1510," trans. E. Theodore Bachmann; Philadelphia edition, Vol. I, "Discussion of Confession (1520)," intro. H. E. Jacobs, 75–80; trans C. M. Jacobs, 81–102; and Philadelphia edition, Vol. VI, "A Short Method of Confessing . . . (1529)," trans. and intr. P. Z. Strodach, 213–16.

25. *Lutheran Book of Worship*, 193.

26. Robert Jenson, "Quod Supra Nos Nihil Ad Nos," *Lutheran Theological Seminary Bulletin* (Winter 1981): 33–41.

27. Nebe, *Luther as Spiritual Advisor*, 114.

28. Ibid., 211.

29. Although written as a novel, the following work gives good insight into the model of spiritual care: Bo Giertz, *The Hammer of God*, reprint (Minneapolis: Augsburg Publishing House, 1973). See also part 2 of Olof Hartman, *Earthly Things* (Grand Rapids: Wm. B. Eerdmans, 1968); and John Doberstein, *Minister's Prayer Book* (Philadelphia: Muhlenberg Press, 1959), which outlines the approach through a masterful anthology of readings from predominantly German, Puritan English, and early American writers.

30. William Hulme's *Counseling and Theology* (Minneapolis: Augsburg Publishing House, 1959), was the classic bridge between older and newer models; cf. also Walter Koehler, *Counseling and Confession* (St. Louis: Concordia Publishing House, 1982).

31. Hermann Dietzfelbinger, quoted in Doberstein, *Minister's Prayer Book*, 320.

32. Cf. Dietrich Bonhoeffer, *The Cost of Discipleship*, trans. Reginald H. Fuller (New York: Macmillan Co., 1960), chap. 1.

33. Cf. Luther's Large Catechism, sub Commandment One; and see also Paul Tillich, *Dynamics of Faith* (London: George Allen & Unwin, 1957), 48–52, on "broken myth."

34. Abraham Joshua Heschel, *God in Search of Man* (New York: Harper & Row, 1965), 30.

Spiritual Care _____

I. THE MISSION OF
SPIRITUAL CARE

The mission of spiritual care falls under the general mission of proclamation. Caring for the soul is a special sort of proclamation. The minister should proclaim wherever possible. The minister is the pastor, that is, the shepherd of the congregation which needs daily care (2 Tim. 4:2). "Preach the word, be urgent in season and out of season, convince, rebuke, and exhort, be unfailing in patience and in teaching." Caring for souls is a proclamation to the individual which is part of the office of preaching. It is not a matter of "spiritual direction"; Asmussen's concept[1] is misleading. In confidence that God alone cares for the soul, the preacher conducts spiritual care. "Spiritual direction" is carried out on a plane between two people, one of whom subjects himself to the other. Spiritual care, on the other hand, comes down "from above," from God to the human being. For this reason the New Testament teaches reverence for the "Teacher" (Heb. 13:7). Spiritual direction is a task of educating the populace carried out by the "priest of the people." In spiritual care, God wants to act. In the midst of all anxiety and sorrow we are to trust God. God alone can be a help and a comfort. The goal of spiritual care should never be a change of mental condition. The mission itself is the decisive element, not the goal. All false hope and every false comfort must be eliminated. I do not provide *decisive* help for anyone if I turn a sad person into a cheerful one, a timid person into a courageous one. That would be a secular—and not a real—help. Beyond and within circumstances such as sadness and timidity it should be believed that God is our help and comfort. Christ and his victory over health and sickness, luck and misfortune, birth and death must be proclaimed. The help he brings is forgiveness and new life out of death.

30

Spiritual care is part of a special mission within *diakonia*. It is related to the office of proclamation but not identical to it. The diaconate of spiritual care arises from a specific problem of proclamation: a person is no longer able to hear the gospel. The more often a person hears it, the more he withdraws from the living Word. Repentance turns into its opposite, into impenitence and callousness. One hears and yet does not hear. One receives and yet is not helped. God's forgiveness is not accepted but the person learns how to deal with himself gracefully. Forgiveness is taken into one's own hands. A special *diakonia* is needed in order to bring people (who have become callous) back to the arena of proclamation. A love is needed which will lead people back to hearing the proclamation of the gospel. This *diakonia* itself cannot be an act of preaching. Spiritual care presumes the previous proclamation of the gospel and moves toward a future proclamation. Spiritual care as a *diakonia* is thus different from that spiritual care which takes place in and through preaching. In this process of spiritual care as *diakonia* the pastor's task is to listen and the parishioner's is to talk. The pastor's duty in this form of spiritual care may be to be silent for a long time in order to become free of all "priestly" behavior and conceited clericalism. That silence, which is the unconditional prerequisite for spiritual care, aids our preaching, for only after a long period of listening is one able to preach appropriately.

There are objections to this distinction between spiritual care as preaching or proclamation and spiritual care as a *diakonia*: *diakonia* as described above is only half the service rendered. It takes the ultimacy out of preaching. Only proclamation (it will be objected) can lead to hearing the proclamation—that is correct. The sermon remains the encompassing element of spiritual care. But sinfulness renders this hearing ineffective; human nature moves toward self-justification. Sin is, in every instance, something quite concrete. It must be recognized and identified by name. Only the demon which is called by name departs.[2] The word of grace cannot be proclaimed and accepted when a person lives in unrecognized and undisclosed sin.[3] In such a case the word of grace becomes a poison. It no longer arouses us but rather lulls us into a deadly quietism. When the effect of the poison has worn off, one still has a disconsolate conscience. Impenitence and callousness become more firmly entrenched. Countless Christians hear the word of grace only in this way. For them it has become a sleeping pill. The person is cheated out of a salutary life in awe of God.

Spiritual care as *diakonia* is necessary: a) because a person grows callous toward hearing the Gospel through unknown and secret sins; b) because the sermon from time to time only strengthens impenitence. Wanton sinfulness depends on this "grace" and thus leads to what the Roman Catechism calls "the sin against the Holy Spirit"; c) because the sermon cannot call sins by name and thus is powerless to expel them; d) because the oral expression of the parishioner is essential but it does not transpire in the sermon.

Thus spiritual care joins with the sermon to enable this person to uncover and banish true sin. This definition of spiritual care applies equally to sick and to healthy people, to the troubled and to the complacent, to sinners and to the righteous. It is a *diakonia* to the congregation which serves the end of proclamation. It springs from the sermon and leads one back to the sermon. It protects against the specific danger of Protestantism, which is to turn the justification of sinners into the justification of sin.[4]

The mission of spiritual care is given especially to the pastor as a ordained preacher of the gospel. But this form of spiritual care is also to be entrusted to elders who have a charisma for this type of *diakonia*. This *diakonia*, therefore, depends on the universal priesthood. The universal priesthood is based on faith, the office on a commission.[5] The office is not derived from the universal priesthood. The pastoral proclamation lies with those who hold office, the *diakonia* to spiritual care lies with the universal priesthood, of which the pastor is also a member. Rightly understood, spiritual care has a pedagogical character; but in service to the gospel its only goal can be new and right hearing of the sermon.[6] Spiritual care does not want to bring about competence, build character, or produce certain types of persons.[7] Instead it uncovers sin and creates hearers of the gospel.

II. LAW AND GOSPEL IN
SPIRITUAL CARE

Law and Gospel are as much a part of spiritual care as they are of proclamation. Spiritual care prepares people to hear the law as God's commandment and to hear the gospel as actual deliverance and help. How can spiritual care do this? How do we speak to the person who is no longer able to hear the word of God in faith?[8]

To a great extent it has become customary to expect from spiritual care and proclamation not faith and salvation but advice and aid in any kind of emergency. We cannot allow this to continue. This is an avoidance of the gospel even and especially when the person in question participates in worship. As a rule this happens because the person is unwilling to give himself to the Word of God without reservation, to trust and obey the Word. There is a kind of natural acknowledgment of God's lordship over our lives. But when it comes to turning over to God a very concrete area and a definite decision, we deny that to him. Precisely this one item, maybe *only* this one we want to withhold from God. God is not to rule in this particular area. And we do not notice that in this way we deny God lordship over our lives in general. The *whole* person is judged by God and it is a whole person that God claims anew. The withholding of specific parts of our own nature, of our vocation, and of our social life gradually delivers us into tight imprisonment. This condition is experienced as distress, but not understood as sin. This condition can lead to total indifference toward proclamation. The word of forgiveness is invariably a concrete word for concrete sins. If I do not want to hear it concretely because I want to retain this part of my life for myself, I cannot hear the word of forgiveness at all. For every other area in my life I soon turn the Word of God into a drug—and one soon tires of drugs as a rule. The grace of God becomes, in the end, reduced to the grace I grant to myself.

The pastor must know what is at stake in this situation. The human will does not want to bow before the will of God. One becomes spiteful, callous, and unrepentant toward God. People accuse God; they ask why God has burdened them with this sickness, this death, this failure, this marital problem. The crucial question behind all these problems is whether or not God's Word is being accepted as God's Word. Time and again one meets with a great "innocence" regarding the seriousness of the command to obedience. It must always be clear to the pastor that the core of the "problem" is flight from the Word of God. As long as we evade and justify our sins, we must be confronted with the hard law. The principle, "sin boldly," applies only when a person is driven to despair.

The pastor as spiritual curate is better informed about others than they are about themselves. The pastor understands the latter's questions correctly and hears through the uncovered need or problem a confession of sin which is not yet risked. Thus a conversation in spiritual care can and must from the start aim toward the other person's alienation. It must become clear that everything necessary for our help is to be found in the Word of God and that it is essential for us to listen to the Word. The person must be brought back to the path of proclamation from which he strayed in impenitence over a quite specific sin. "Go to Church!"—"I don't get anything out of it!" "You don't want to listen."—"I want to but I can't." The pastoral question presses further: "Why do you deny Christ obedience at this particular point in your life? As long as you do this consciously at this point, of course you can't hear. The anxiety you express is in reality your sin." In this sentence "your anxiety is your sin" lies the decisive starting point for spiritual care. It is imperative to move from the question that breaks out of an earthly or natural stress situation to the distress of sin. This is particularly important in pastoral conversation with young people. With them most questions are but a pretext. So we shouldn't take the question put forth with dead seriousness, but of course we must take seriously the one who has asked the question. His question hides his situation. He sketches his anxiety but does not confess sin. We must move from pretext to the central issue. Suggested changes in lifestyle are not much help; only God's offer of forgiveness can come as help.

The "rich young man" (Matt. 19:16–26) comes to Jesus because of an alleged burning religious problem. The "good master" should answer his question about eternal life. Jesus offers the questioner no help in regard to the stated problem. He should keep the commandments and practice simple, straightforward obedience. When he seeks escape in the multiplicity of the commandments, Jesus shows him that obedience is decisive in one point.[10] With this the disease of argumentation is repudiated as dangerous. It arises from the withholding of simple obedience. Fleeing the Word of God, one submerges himself in problems in order to evade simple obedience. Jesus pits the clarity of the commandments against the opacity of the problems.

In spiritual care, therefore, one takes seriously the questioners as those who stand before God as sinners. For this reason one must not take the questions too seriously so long as they cover or hide this situation. We do not help a mourner who rebels against God because of a death by taking the defiance seriously. We will be able to say in only a few circumstances that the dead person is with God and thereby saved. We have no comfort. Only God can fill in the hole by breaking in upon a life. Comfort comes only when God becomes more important to the mourner than anything else, including questions about the fate of the dead.

Those trapped in vice are not healed by being hit with advice. The flesh is strong. It loves a good argument. But people will never relinquish the enjoyment of their sins even when outwardly they seem to be seeking our advice. Only surrender to Christ and joyful discipleship are able to spring us free of the bonds of sin.

It is similar with a sick person, who loves the condition of sickness. He enjoys being comforted and frequently takes pleasure in his need. He seeks human counsel that will support his psychological condition and soothe him. He loves discussion. But as soon as the advice turns into a commandment, or God's Word cuts off his word, he will start to argue. Then he won't want to listen anymore. When no argument arises we should probably be afraid we've spoken only human counsel instead of God's Word. The proper end of all this conversation is confession, in the shortest and simplest form. Then distress will no longer be the topic of conversation but sin.

Spiritual care as *diakonia* thus follows the pathway from counsel to commandment, from expression of need to confession of sin, from speech to hearing the promise. It is a path of familial assistance toward hearing the proclamation. The proclamation must not jump over all the preliminary stages. Should we oppose the question immediately with the commandment, we're likely to hear, "I can't." The pure commandment does not help the situation but rather hardens it. The other person must be helped along the path from recognition of sin and confession to voluntary obedience and faith. The questioner is to be led to ask for God's commandment. In this way, opposition to God turns to submission.

The path of spiritual care as *diakonia* has its presuppositions:

No pastoral conversation is possible without constant prayer. Other people must know that I stand before God as I stand before them. I depend on the guidance of the Holy Spirit. There is no immediate path to another person. The path to the Christian brother leads by way of prayer and hearing God's Word. No psychology is able to help me find the way to another person's soul. That path is grounded in the mediatorial function of Christ. Christ the mediator stands between me and God, between me and my brother. Therefore, spiritual care never seeks to exercise direct psychic influence. Direct influence remains wholly on the surface. True encounter is only facilitated through the spirit of Christ. The other person must deal with Christ if he is to be helped. Even my piety is useless. The only imprint he should and can receive is that one which is in accordance with the *imago Dei*. That way we keep the atmosphere clear between us and others. The direct path contains deliberations and suggestions, but they leave the other person to himself. What I am able to do for another person will be shown me in prayer.[11] Prayer commends the others into the faithful hands of Christ and Christ will deal with them. In order to pray correctly, we must be able to listen to the other person.[12] Those who cannot hear another person are also no longer able to hear God's Word . . . or to pray! Our love for another consists first of all in listening.

The pastor who will never confront the other person in a calculating or investigative manner has long experience with what is essential. The other person is a sinner whom God's mercy wants to encounter. That is the difference between spiritual care and psychotherapy, for which the method of investigation is all-important. Spiritual care puts no stock in such methods. There are no "psychologically interesting cases" for spiritual care; to approach the matter in such a way would be a disavowal of the office. What is supposed to be learned that is new beyond sin? The pastor remains fundamentally premethodical and prepsychological, in the best sense naïve. Otherwise spiritual care could get to the point where magic and daimonism begin to take precedence over the purity and simplicity of familial love. The psychic connects to magical powers. The psychic seeks immediacy in the encounter of two souls. In psychoanalysis the "doctor complex" occurs after the first phase; one becomes dependent on this particular doctor. Although in a later stage of analysis one tries to reduce this complex, the solution never quite solves anything; we wind up with a different form of dependence. The pastor, on the other hand, does not bind anyone to himself at any stage, but only to the Word and Spirit of Christ. Where people try to enter into dependence on the pastor, the pastor must be firm and resistant without being unkind. The uneasy atmosphere of psychic immediacy must not be allowed to enter into spiritual care. The pastor loves the other person so much as to risk being hated by the other. Through dependency on Word, prayer, and faith the other person is freed from bondage to his own ego.

The true pastor will certainly ask investigative questions but only in order to get the person to talk. The immodest manner of interrogation is eliminated by familial love. The pastor only wants to know in order to help. Afterward he quickly forgets what he knows. Naiveté serves a better purpose than the dark magic of exercising control. Other people are to be placed before God alone and, through God, their eyes are to be opened.[13]

Despite the immediacy of attachment, distance is still maintained between doctor and patient in psychotherapy. This happens because the patient submits to the doctor's knowledge and ability and thus feels dependent on the doctor. The doctor is comparable to a magician. The distance between pastor and parishioner is of another order. It is not based on differing gifts and personal powers but on the office God has given the pastor. Fundamentally there is no difference at all between pastor and parishioner. The pastor comes empty-handed like all others. It is a distance into which God places a seeker with a helper. It is not a question of power relationships but of a difference in commission. All questions of personal worthiness are beside the point and put us in the realm of psychotherapy. To those who come to us for spiritual care our ability has less than no authority. Only the mission binds us and calls us together. The pastor as spiritual curate is not a person of unusual experience, ability, or maturity. He should not pass himself off as such, as a "person you can trust," "a priestly person," or the like. If he does, he will only put himself in Jesus' place and arouse expectations he will of necessity disappoint. People will most likely confide in us. But they ought rather place their trust in the Word, Christ, alone. To this end we can serve and aid. The more they turn to Christ the less will we steer any attention to ourselves.

It would certainly be most misleading to remove the distance between pastor and parishioner which is established by God's commission.[14] The pastor should not—out of a misguided idea of solidarity—speak about personal unworthiness or sin. As a rule this is not helpful for the other person. By doing this, we interpose ourselves and our own problems between the other person and Christ. It could also be an evasion of the mission of spiritual care. The relationship may proceed naturally to the point where one doesn't know who is pastor and who is parishioner. But we shouldn't make a method of that which is an ultimate possibility and a genuine grace. The office of spiritual care does not exist to declare solidarity but to listen and to proclaim the gospel. Proper distance helps establish proper closeness.

The pastor can learn very little from the psychologist, basically only to observe, to evaluate, and to analyze. That is certainly not decisive for his service.[15] His service consists of bringing people to God and to salvation. The best pastor is the one who loves Christ. So there will arise between the pastor and the other person a pure, clear love for God and for humanity. I expect naught from myself, everything from the work of Christ. My service has its objectivity in that expectation and by it I am freed from all anxiety about my insufficiency and failure.

Only meditation and struggle with the cross are able to impel spiritual care.[16] With such a background we will no more be shocked no matter how great the sin. At the cross of Christ we learn to see ourselves and others as sinners. What sin can be greater than the godlessness which Christ took to the cross? We show an impoverished understanding of the cross of Christ if we are "shocked" by a great sin which we learn about, for example, in confession. These are the realities all of us deal with as sinners. At the cross of Christ we learn to look such things in the eye and in this process become aware of our nearness to others. In contrast to this, the psychotherapist, even if he grounds himself as much as possible on the reality of sin, remains for the other person (1) too distant, since he wants to overcome evil by his own powers; (2) too close, since he is too immediate in his relationship to the sick person; and (3) too erotic, since he—in distinction from the love of Christ—builds only on human relations.

Spiritual care in the congregation must not be limited to one-time encounters. The pastor often accompanies the other person on pilgrimage silently and wordlessly, but at all times as intercessor.[17] The other person ought to know this. In order to be able to carry on the ministry of intercession the pastor should free specific times in the daily routine. In prayer for the congregation, intercession is taken for granted. Intercession for individuals is harder. But it must not become sporadic and thus it may be enabled best through a specific ritual. It is immaterial who breaks the silence. As a rule, it will be the pastor.

One should not change pastors arbitrarily when under spiritual care.[18] The congregation should hold to its appointed pastor in spiritual care as in preaching if no serious grounds speak against doing so. Such a ground would be notorious heresy, false teaching, or irresponsibility in the conduct of the office, such as a breach of the confessional seal. But it should never be mere inhibition before one who knows us well or with whom we fear losing our moral prestige. Felix Timmermann, in "The Farmer's Psalm," tells of a farmer who would not confess his adultery to the parish pastor. He waited until a revival came to the area and confessed to the preacher who was from outside the area. What happened was that the absolution did not really touch his conscience and so he wound up going at last to his own pastor. Evasion before the pastor is most of the time an evasion of spiritual care. The inevitable question of confidentiality is adequately answered with reference to one's respect for the confessional seal. Apart from that it should not play too great a role. Trust in or to another person must not become the central issue in spiritual care. If it does become central, then the necessary objectivity gets lost. In this respect the contemporary Protestant church is in bad shape. We will be able to regain our objectivity only by reflecting anew on the confessional seal and on its concomitant secrecy.

Great spiritual gifts or rich life experience do not predispose anyone to the service of spiritual care, but love of Christ does. Love of Christ makes one wise. "I understand more than the aged, for I keep thy precepts" (Ps. 119:100). Augustine did not receive his knowledge of people through his own experience, but through Christ and his love for him. Love alone enables us to communicate deep self-understanding to others.

Spiritual care occurs between two people. Marital problems are on occasion the exception to this rule. Spiritual care does not put up with observers, thus one can learn it from others only with great difficulty. One has to gain one's own experiences. Once the tongue is loosened in spiritual conversation, it won't often be silent again. The act of confession can easily turn into exhibitionism. Such instincts must not be unleashed or strengthened. Any "Christian" exhibitionism must be guarded against from the beginning. Spiritual care is quite modest.

Discretion in the conduct of the pastoral office is the uppermost commandment. In ordination this is laid upon us as a duty. The pastor keeps quiet about everything he learns in the exercise of the office. The pastor conducts spiritual care alone; spouses are excluded from it. That constitutes a great sacrifice for the spouse, who is not permitted to participate in a broad and important area of experience in the life of the pastor. Spouses should be compensated for this sacrifice in some other way. This discretion toward everyone, including one's spouse, should be mentioned on occasion in a wedding homily to encourage young people to take advantage of spiritual care. Discretion does not preclude that a pastor might seek the counsel of other ordained pastors for special emergencies and inform them of the issues as far as necessary.

Every word the pastor says about the congregation should be carefully weighed. The congregation is not the pastor's topic of conversation, but rather it is the flock of Christ to which he has been commissioned by his office and his responsibility. Whenever he does not observe this rule, he will find himself the congregation's topic of conversation! The pastor must also not discuss other pastors with the congregation. Gossip is usually the worst evil in a congregation. Gossip poisons all trust and destroys all constructive work. The parsonage must be the one place in the congregation in which others are not talked about. And the congregation must be able to trust that this is so in that house. The pastor should not pass up the opportunity to preach from time to time about the evils of the tongue. If the pastor is not discreet in small things then why would anyone entrust him with important matters in the confessional? Observing the confessional seal is but the ultimate point of a total demeanor.

The confessional seal is a divine commandment. Its breach must result in loss of office. In the confessional the salvation of the soul is at stake. The other person only confides in me and puts himself in my hands because I act "in God's stead." I must keep this secret as God keeps it. No worldly power must be allowed to tear it from me. God will require the soul of the confessor from the one who reveals the confidences made in the confessional. The government takes this into account by guaranteeing the seal of confession to the pastor under public law. The one who confesses should also keep the confessional seal. Only on the day of judgment will what was spoken in the confessional be revealed.

Spiritual care that leads from advice to proclamation begins with the preceding suppositions. The loosing and binding Word is only able to come at the end. What now is the concrete course of this path of spiritual care? We must bring the other person to speech. One must find the point at which he has become indifferent to God's Word. For this purpose the area indicated by the Ten Commandments is to be checked. Even here the danger of evading the actual sin persists, because a pretense will be offered. Perhaps the other person has for so long lied to himself that he must now lie to the pastor. Much error and hiding will often come to light, as well as our fault for letting the other person become so impenitent. We have left the person alone. We will discover the reason for impenitence where the other person is no longer able to perceive the direct commandment of God.

Pastoral work begins here. If, for instance, a fight with parents or in the marriage is at stake, reminding the person of the fourth and sixth commandments is worthless. The reply would only be: I can't get out of this predicament. To speak at this point about the seriousness of the commandment and the danger of condemnation would lead only to greater hardening. You have to take a risky step here. The "I can't" is often a psychophysical matter; it must be totally or unconditionally turned around. We must find the point at which the other person can at least make a partial beginning to change the destructive relationship under his own power. A father who is difficult and unpleasant is well served when he is shown that he can change his attitude by his own power. Where I know that I *can*, where the "impossible" is conquered, I am freed from that which stands between me and the commandment. I surmise that the "I can't" means, at bottom, "I won't." "I can't" reveals an accusation against the Creator, since I appropriate to myself the right to make an exception to God's judgment. With the words "I cannot do otherwise" I declare adultery, for example, as my nature and also as my own good law. If it is clear to me at one point that I can do otherwise if I want to, the opposition to the commandment is removed. I have the freedom to hear it. I am delivered without protection to the brunt of the commandment. The net of my excuses is torn open. The paralyzing sense of inner slavery is taken away when I hear "You can." We must encourage the person and point the way through discipline and practice.

Matters are more difficult with the second commandment than with the fourth and sixth: "I can't pray anymore." One might suggest, first of all (avoiding the idea that the suggestion is a commandment), "Do it anyway. Take your time, rest, and be patient. Otherwise you show that you don't want to." All such admonitions, however, are preliminaries to proper spiritual care. These things are profane counsel, which can be risky and dangerous. But such admonitions are necessary preparation for hearing God's Word. They are a help exclusive of the Word so that the Word might be heard.

Finally, beyond the counsel offered, the commandment emerges. This may not happen until all the human presuppositions have been made. We should not undersell or obscure the Word to anyone. They will become weary of such words and throw them back as an accusation at the one who has spoken them. Proclamation of the commandment to an individual presses toward concreteness, toward a singular decision. Proclamation is a concrete instruction by which one is bound to the first commandment.[19] It must be clear that the commandment doesn't relate to isolated or self-evident matters, but rather concerns the whole person; we are not talking about a general divinity but about the whole God in relation to a human being. It is the *gracious* God who seeks a person through this first commandment. Joy and thanksgiving are instilled since, in the commandment, God as gracious God is with us.[20]

How do I find this commandment? We do not wait in such moments for some special enlightenment, but rather turn, wholly sober, to the Scriptures in prayer and familial love and then risk a decision. The commandment does not have a solitary criterion; the commandment is a risk, like the use of the office of the keys.[21] Error is not precluded. But the one who gives spiritual care must take that error upon himself and take responsibility for the correctness of a judgment concerning the other person. What is left to the other person, of course, is obedience. The pastor is liable, the other person is free . Without such a deep intervention in another life, nothing will ever happen in spiritual care.

This intervention is above all called for in the case of total impenitence. When all other attempts run aground, the way back to the Word remains. The concreteness of the Word shows itself in the threat of divine judgment to those who will not hear the commandment. We are speaking here of a dissolution of divine judgment to those who will not hear the commandment. We are speaking here of a dissolution of all standards in a situation and of deliberate uncertainty on principle. Uncertainty *on principle* is always an act of disobedience. It arises in a double form, either as libertine indifference or as moralistic self-torture concerning the right path to take. Never to "arrive at a knowledge of the truth" is always an expression of sinful conduct (2 Tim. 3:7). Those who want to persist in sin will no longer recognize the truth. God does not withhold this truth from them—God wants to make it plain!—but they will not be obedient. They take pleasure in making problems. They hear no word without lots of reflection. Everything becomes disjointed: "Hath God said . . . ?"[22] Only the proclamation of a specific commandment alleviates this situation; only the commandment proclaimed as *grace* can conquer perplexity. It may not help to solve the human difficulties but it can save the soul. To that end alone may I risk and respond with the concrete commandment.

Particular attention must be paid to law and gospel in spiritual care. It goes without saying that one begins with the law in a concrete case. Sin is what blocks people from a fruitful hearing of the Word. General confessions of sin count for little as a rule; they remain unconnected to the power of obedience.[23] As a consequence, we become doubtful; we think it is all self-deception and we really offer forgiveness to ourselves. The other possibility is that we will deal too easily with grace: *"Dieu pardonnera, car tel est son metier"* (Voltaire: "God forgives because that is God's business"). The first of these two denials of obedience leads to *despair*, the second to *security*, and the second is by far the more dangerous.

What must happen so that we don't turn justification of the sinner into justification of the sin? There are two options. The first proceeds from a confession of sin which is made in spiritual care settings and will not be referred to again. Absolution follows the confession; that conforms to the gospel. The presupposition of genuine repentance is made. Otherwise everything may become a pious delirium. A false absolution can destroy the salvation of a Christian's soul.

The second option is the path of assurance of pardon where genuine remorse exists. The section about the renunciation of the devil in the rite of baptism may be helpful here. There is the risk, however, that one may cheat in claiming sincerity of remorse; but who knows his own heart and yet remains silent if this were the case? It would not be right to make the declaration of forgiveness dependent on testing the genuineness of a person's remorse. As before, the first way can lead to a deceptive *security* and the second to a form of *despair*.

What can be done in this event? How can we find help? In general, this is what the law/gospel dialectic is for. The law must be preached just so that law does not lead to *despair*. The gospel must be preached just so that gospel does not lead to *security*. The same is true of obedience and forgiveness; the two must remain tightly connected with each other. Forgiveness without obedience leads one to a facile dealing with grace.[24] The demand for obedience without (a proclamation of) forgiveness would drive a person to perplexity. Only he who is obedient believes. Only he who is faithful obeys. There is a principle here for spiritual care: *the law must be contained in the gospel, and the gospel must be contained in the law.*

It follows that there is also a relationship between penitence and forgiveness. The prodigal in Luke 15, who knows himself to be lost, is accepted again by the father. That is to say, the one who is ready to repent finds forgiveness. Penitence and forgiveness are so closely tied that one can reverse the principle: only he who is forgiven finds his way to penitence. Only he who is penitent receives the kingdom of heaven, and only because the kingdom of heaven has come near is there repentance. Law and gospel coexist into eternity. The word of Jesus to the adulteress in John 8:11, "Neither do I condemn you: go, and do not sin again," seems to contradict that statement. Here the gospel seems to come before the law. But in reality they coexist. In any event, that is how it happens in spiritual care. The law cannot be offered without the gospel and vice versa. By paying attention to both of them, law and gospel, others are led back to Word and Sacrament.

The pastor must keep in mind that *disobedience*, as well as obedience, has the power to transform a person completely. Through disobedience in a particular decision, one can falsify the whole sequence of right thinking. The pastoral epistles talk about this a lot. Disobedience comes in a variety of disguises: as superficial indifference or as the continuous creation of problems; as ascetic rigorism or as sectarianism; as the quest for novelty or as a philosophical restlessness. All that stuff is given a lot of weight preeminently to cover a scar in the conscience that lies hidden in the background. There is a great deal to be learned in the pastoral epistles about spiritual care.

Evasions of this kind will recur again and again. People do not mind being sick or bogged down with problems or even weak—but under no conditions do they want to be sinners. We do not mind saying a formula that we are "altogether sinful"—but a formula doesn't trouble our consciences. On the contrary, the formula is advantageous as a final excuse and a last attempt at evasion. Therefore, concrete sins must come to the light of day.

A goal of all concerns in spiritual care is to accept the partner in conversation as a sinner. Consolation and confrontation must be continually made in their proper relation to law and gospel. For theological reflection, everything the Lutheran Confessions say about confession is of great importance.

III. HOME VISITATION

In a visit to the home, the pastor goes without the trappings afforded by chancel, altar, or vestment. In no other place will he be less able to hide behind objectivity. The congregation must inform the pastor that he has *one* concern, the proclamation of the gospel. He may have a lot of other interests but they do not belong in conversations concerned with spiritual care. A parishioner must be able to sense that the pastor's words overflow out of the fullness of his heart. They can tell if our proclamation is a spiritual reality for us. The pastor who cannot pray extemporaneously or to whom spiritual care is slightly objectionable should not expect a parishioner to make the first move in the relationship. Every unsuccessful pastoral visit is a difficult judgment against us, because it will display our lack of spiritual experience and power. Every pastoral visit requires spiritual preparation which proceeds from the open Bible and from prayer. What we have read in the morning, if we took it seriously, will and should turn up in our conversations.[25] It is often helpful to envision a specific text as a central focus. Generally speaking, a visit in which there is no resort to either Scripture or prayer will be unfruitful. We would like to shove the blame for an unsuccessful visit on the people, on their lack of preparation to discuss spiritual verities. But as a rule, we are to blame. Many a pastor does not become a true Christian until he engages in spiritual care.

For the Roman Church, the locus for spiritual care has been the confessional booth. Home visits have only a preparatory character for the priest. The evangelical pastor shows through a visit that Christ wishes to come to this house. The ordinary, everyday person is the one who is called to a decision for Christ. Christ himself came into homes, to Simon and Andrew (Mark 1:29); to Mary and Martha (Luke 10:38–42); to Zaccheus the tax collector (Luke 19:5–6); and even to the pharisee Simon (Luke 7:35ff). He sent his disciples into homes (Matt. 10:12). Lydia and the Philippian jailor received the Apostle [Paul] in their homes (Acts 16). According to the New Testament, the home is a spiritual reality. Here faith grows and is watched over. Before we step into a strange home we must freely consider that here we will find the other wholly as himself, in his order or his chaos, in the circle of family and friends, at work, among his trappings and symbols. Here the other is ruler and judge, not the pastor. One doesn't allow just anyone to step into his house. No one can claim that right. There are other places where the sanctity of the home is better respected than in Germany; for example, in England the police are not allowed to enter a private home without a search warrant. That the pastor may do this must be reckoned in every way as an extension of trust. It is a special privilege that comes with the office. Therefore the pastor doesn't visit as an observer who finally gets to cast furtive and curious glances upon the secrets of another, but as one who looks upon the scene with modesty and reserve. Now, since the other person discloses how he is when he is at home, and since an acquaintance with someone's home offers lots of contextual information, utmost reserve is called for. The pastor never speaks about what he has seen in a home. That would be a breach of confidence. That pastor should not feel at home too quickly in another's house. Let him never forget that he is a guest. Let him speak accordingly. The other person's house stands as a boundary line for the pastor.[26]

After we reflect on these preliminaries, the peculiar responsibility of the pastor should be clear. What he sees should help him serve and love the other person better. The pastor leads the conversation but he should never forget where he is. He must not abuse his position. Learning about the home will be a *cautious* part of the first conversation. He will however be on guard against the gossip in the home. He is never a friend but a pastor to the family. He must keep foremost the question, how can Christ dwell in this home? He may sometimes ask if family devotions are held; or if and what the children pray; if people attend church and if not, why not? He has no time for small talk, but he always has time to serve.

Even the first visit is aimed at essentials. The congregation must know in advance when the pastor goes into its homes. One preparatory step might be to speak from the chancel about what a visit to the home entails. On the third or fourth visit you may have trouble getting folks to hear the Word. But one shouldn't wait for a favorable opportunity to give the conversation a "spiritual bent." It is better to cut off conversation and to ask if a scriptural text might be read by all. Bible reading and prayer should be part of the pastor's visits in homes.[27] Whether or not such things are taken for granted by the congregation will depend on whether or not the pastor has clarified what he expects from visits and what the parishioners should expect in the way of spiritual care. Situations will occur in which it will not be possible to read the Bible or pray. The pastor should cut such visits short and say that he will return, Bible in hand, for some common reading if that would be all right. Congregations that are unfamiliar with this kind of spiritual care will show their surprise. That should not stop us from pursuing this kind of care. One's pastoral bearing should be self-evident, calm, and impartial at all times. Our service is performed as a command of Christ. If we show partiality then those we visit will do so even more. The more impartial we are, the more grateful the congregation will become in a relatively short time. There are houses in which no "child of peace" (Luke 10:6) dwells. It is not constructive to read scripture or to pray in such situations. Such cases will occur less often than we imagine, however. Better offer too much than too little! Christ cannot come near very often without making the doors open suddenly.

In congregations of northern France, the evangelical pastor goes through the streets with a large Bible tucked under his arm when he makes house calls. That is helpful because then everyone knows what's going on in the visitation.

It is advisable to follow a proper sequence in congregational visitation. First one should visit the elders (presbyters), and then the sick and the poor. At worship, the pastor may ask for notification when someone is sick. That way the congregation shares responsibility for the visitation. The superstitious fear one often encounters that the pastor only calls when the sick are about to die should be dispelled in sermons. Apart from those named above, in large cities the pastor should also visit the parents of confirmands. There is a large task for a circle of assistants (a "visitation-service") in home visitation. Above all, one must give some fundamental instruction about what an office *(Amt)* is in the Christian congregation. Better to send no one to a house than one unprepared! This kind of service can also make the point that Christ comes into the home with the visitor. Visits to the sick and the poor should be frequent and, if possible, always at the same time. One who waits mustn't be disappointed!

A special problem: houses where folks want to tie up the pastor through frequent invitations. The pastor has a right to social intercourse and to friendship. But one ought to consider how far he should make use of this right within the congregation. The same thing goes for the right to play and pleasure. He doesn't belong in bars at all (particularly to be seen in the parish!). He can give offense by such behavior. The main thing in such concerns is not to make one's service as a witness to Jesus Christ more difficult or unbelievable.

IV. CONVERSATIONS WITH THE INDIFFERENT

Perhaps it would be better to speak of the undecided rather than the indifferent. There are three different modes of indecision which we should not confuse with one another:

First mode: there are people who receive such fulfillment through vocation and family that they lack nothing. They are satisfied, content, and fortunate. They attend church sporadically when it suits them or they feel the need for some celebration. They live *alongside* the church.

Second mode: these are the educated and cultured folk who are above ecclesiastical things. As one is above school and teacher, so is one above church and pastor. They are angry with the narrow-mindedness of the church and the partial education of the pastor. They deem some bits of knowledge from the philosophy of religion worthwhile. The educated stand on one hand next to the church, on the other hand they stand *over* the church. Perhaps today [1935–1938!—trans.] they feel that they will never again find their way into a real church.

Third mode: these are the callous, the discontented, the disappointed, who miss no opportunity for anger against church and pastor. They stand *against* the church.

Regarding the first mode: one needs to state clearly that a place next to the church isn't possible. Indecision is, in large measure, untruthfulness. The pastor must therefore press for a decision pro or con. The conversation might go somewhat as follows: "Why don't you attend church?" "I don't need it. My religious needs are satisfied elsewhere, in nature or at a concert." "No religious needs are ultimately satisfied, however, apart from Christ." "I have nothing against Christ; I'm a Christian." "Do you know what Christ longs for? Either a complete yes or a complete no. As an individual you've long since said no to him. You are fascinated by him but you distance yourself from him whenever he draws too close. You are against Christ. 'He who is not with me is against me' (Matt. 12:30). You have to start anew with Christ. If you do that, then you'll be with those who take Christ seriously. It's not a question of satisfying religious needs but of living with Christ. One only has Christ in the congregation and in the church. If you are for Christ, then you must also be for the church."

This kind of indecisive person should also be addressed concerning his inner poverty: "For you say, I am rich, I have prospered, and I need nothing; not knowing that you are wretched, pitiable, poor, blind, and naked" (Rev. 3:17). It is not out of place to remind people that one is foolish to consider a momentary state of contentment as permanent. "You fool! This very night your soul will be required of you" (Luke 12:20). Age, sickness, suffering, loneliness, and anxiety will come in any event.[28] One has to bear these things alone if one rejects the community and, with it, Christ. Our speech cannot be clear or assertive enough with this sort of indecisive person. You must eschew all false security. It remains to be said that the conscience of such folk collapses easily and with little thought to a political world view.

Regarding the second mode: the cultured are among the most isolated people of our age. They've become distant from the church through a century-long process of individualization and intellectualization. Their spiritual home is liberalism. But in the last decades even this has offered little ground for a spiritual existence. The air became too thin to sustain life and the foundations were not capable enough. Many people have sensed this or even seen it clearly. In the years since 1933, the foundation of their existence has been completely taken away.[29] They have become, in a unique sense, refugees. Now, surprisingly, many of them felt themselves drawn into the proclamation and struggle of the Confessing church. They sensed that a free space had been won in the Confessing church which could not be found anywhere else anymore. In some way their path was comparable to the tax collectors and sinners in the New Testament who came to Jesus since they found in him a life which was elsewhere denied them. And yet the cultured cannot go along wholly with the Confessing church in an honest way because of their spiritual tradition.[30] In their isolation, their doubt, their external temporizing and their internal loss of foundations, they are the sacrifice of Culture-Protestantism.[31]

Conversation with the cultured tends to be protracted. Much junk has to be cleared out of the way. There aren't many who are in a position to carry on such extended conversation. It is very difficult and demands a lot of tact. Two possibilities present themselves.

Give a personal witness of faith in childlike simplicity unhampered by doubt, criticism, or spiritual superiority! The cultured person must be attentive to that. Only a real spiritual word has credibility. The reaction could go something like this: "If I could only believe once again in a childlike way. But of course we are no longer children."

The other way is to make an understanding entry into his situation. After a lot of silence, the person will at length ask his own questions. The pastor shouldn't say much about himself. His partner will immediately rubricate what he says—he can hardly help it—and then the words lose their effectiveness. The question should be awakened within him, "What's behind this understanding and participation? A lot more than naked curiosity! How can one be so understanding and yet believe all that?" Don't expect overnight success on this path. The roundabout way of philosophical, semireligious conversation is not totally commendable. The pastor can enter it only if he knows the subject matter. The partially educated person who acts as if he knows a lot gets on people's nerves. Candid matter-of-factness and love are a unique witness to the things of Christ. An arrogant tone on the pastor's part is totally devastating. The cultured person's educational ideal includes modest objectivity and a recognition of one's own limits. By such gauges he will measure a pastor. The Christian faith is usually stated poorly in discussions and discourse; its proper setting is proclamation. for this reason Künneth's *Antwort auf den Mythos* [*Answer to Myth*] is not a good book. Where the truth of the gospel is concerned, one proper dose of clumsiness (see Luther!) is more adequate than such attempts at discussion. The pastor should maintain the same distance to philosophical questions that his partner does, just so long as he doesn't discuss things he knows nothing about. He should protect himself from making moralizing judgments like "You cultured people always want to be so clever. You and your Latin!" To criticize the faculty of reason would be the dumbest thing the pastor could do. When the moment to witness arrives, let him speak impartially, confidently, and with certainty about Christ.

Regarding the third mode: where people have taken offense at the discrepancy between word and deed on the part of the church or an individual pastor, the quiet service of love is the best spiritual care.[32] Often these attacks are unjust because pastors do a lot that remains unseen. Often, however, such attacks are justified. The pastor accepts such people even where it concerns their worldly well-being. A small service may do wonders. One has to be a match for these declared critics. Critics must learn that they don't completely understand the ways of the church and that they have a lot to learn. More important than this, however, is the witness of social aid. Everyone understands that. To the complaint, "Yes, this one here is occasionally a good pastor, but those others . . . ," one might counter by saying, "Did you always do your duty when the bad pastor was there?" Spiritual care transcends the medium of the pastor's personality. What's important is this: "having this ministry by the word of God, we do not lose heart" (2 Cor. 4:1). The silent deed may lead to an ingenuous proclamation.

V. SPIRITUAL CARE TO THOSE WHO ARE TEMPTED

There are known and unknown, open and hidden temptations. There is always something to snatch away our faith. Hidden or unknown temptations come slowly and stealthily. One day we notice with surprise how inconsequential God has become to us. We can't figure out where that pathway began. Open or known temptations often come suddenly, shaking us with their enormous force. The devil likes to make use of our times of weakness.

It is important to name three kinds of known temptations:

a. We experience an overwhelming onslaught on our emotions. Ambition, idleness, lusting after power or sex—these things gain power over us. Our clear ability to reckon things is suddenly beclouded. What we earlier recognized as morally wrong seems under these circumstances here and now not to be sinful. "Has God really said . . . ?" This old devil's question distorts God's word in our mouths. Thus Satan is revealed as the liar from the beginning. He carts off our reason in chains, obedient to him and no longer obedient to Christ. In such moments the image of Christ is wholly vanquished. The vision of the crucified one, of his pierced and tortured body, at other times an aid and protection against evil, no longer speaks to us. The image is lost. The one who brings such temptation upon us is none other than "the old evil foe." We have one answer, one salvation: "Depart from me, you liar!"

Through these sudden attacks we fall captive not so much to an uncertainty about salvation but rather to indifference about it. We sell our souls to the devil for a mess of pottage. And know not what we do!

b. Another kind of known temptation is melancholy, *acedia*.[33] In Roman moral theology this is reckoned as the seventh deadly sin.[34] With good reason! Melanchthon was well acquainted with it. Through it a person falls to pieces. It drives him to complete isolation, so that he tells himself life is senseless and gratuitous. Darkness descends between God and the person, so that the person loses God. Melancholy does not stem so much from uncertainty about salvation as from doubt of God's presence *(Dasein)*.[35] The question of salvation never gets asked. The person who is tested by melancholy is a bouncing ball in the devil's hands, given to thoughts of suicide. At times nothing more is desired!

There is a particular danger that *melancholy* will not be considered a sin. On the contrary it may be deemed as quite pious. Melancholy sneaks a peek at the "godly grief" of 2 Cor. 7:10 and would like to be mistaken for it. It's important to see through this illusion as a special stratagem of the devil, who would like to grasp the tempted person in the midst of his lack of trust in God.

c. Finally, with known temptations a direct attack is made upon saving faith. Faith in the salvation wrought by Christ is destroyed. If a person is pained by an anxious conscience he hasn't got his faith straight—his sin is too great to be forgiven; he's committed the sin against the Holy Ghost; he's one of the goats; he's guilty of an unworthy reception of the sacrament. This is temptation in its most proper sense. Luther called it the Christian temptation. The person knows himself to be bound in Satan's power. He is no longer master of his temptation. He feels an angry God standing over him.

The one who provides spiritual care must know that in all these temptations a struggle with Satan is going on. He is not dealing with human weakness but with a demonic "possession" and captivity in Blumhardt's sense. The devil yields to no human attack, whether it be that of our own strength or the art of the psychotherapist. The devil feels at home in such surroundings. Christ must enter the battleground with his clear word. The question that thus comes to expression is, how does the word of Christ become audible in the face of such temptations?

Fleshly temptation has its root in *pride*. The proud flesh excuses itself from the hearing of God's Word. *"Et religio caro est"* (Luther) ("and re-

ligion is made flesh"—a paraphrased translation of the Latin text of
John 1). The flesh must become humble and reverent. Such humility
occurs when we take upon ourselves renunciations and denials. Above
all it happens as we keep the passion of Christ before our eyes. Luther
practiced daily meditation before a picture of the crucified One. Such
meditation needn't happen after the fashion of the medieval mystics or
the almost masochistic excesses of the devotees of Zinzendorf; it can
arise from contemplation of the representative event of the Cross of
Christ.

> "Thy grief and bitter passion
> were all for sinners' gain:
> Mine, mine was the transgression,
> but thine the deadly pain"
> (LBW 116, stanza 2b).

So we must look after our brothers and sisters who are tempted, that
they might fight even when they would like to give in. My defeat is
their defeat, even as conversely my victory gives them aid. The humbled
flesh hears the punitive Word of God, and the punitive Word opens the
pathway once more to the gracious Word.

The gates through which spiritual trial or melancholy invades us are,
first, unthankfulness before God; second, hopelessness in the face of all
God must perform; and third, hidden and unforgiven sins. The first
creates a false attitude toward the past, the second toward the future,
and the third toward the present. The devil must leave by the same gate
through which he entered. When involved in spiritual care with those
whose temptation is melancholy, the pastor must elaborate upon what
God has done in the past, what God will do in the future, and what
God requires in the present.

First: "He who brings thanksgiving as his sacrifice honors me; to him
who orders his way aright, I will show the salvation of God!" (Ps.
50:23). The way out of spiritual trial leads through thanksgiving.
P. Geyser *("Besuch an Sterbebett")* tells of an old dying woman whom he
met who was troubled by doubt. She had, in the past, stood firm in the
faith. But now she declared that she was cast away from God. Consolation from the Bible was to no avail. She already knew all the right
words. Geyser was unable to console her by any means. This same ex-
change went on for days. But then he asked the question, Is there any-

thing unknown in your life? No, she said. Uneventful repetition. On the day she died, he was once more with her. He asked if she had given thanks to God for her life. The woman was unsure. He asked her to pray with him. In a long prayer he uplifted her whole life in thanksgiving. That broke the ice. The thanksgiving that broke out released her from doubt. The missing thanksgiving was the obstruction. The devil had gathered all his power where she felt guilty for not having given thanks. Thus we can truthfully say: when thanksgiving fails all else fails. If there is something in our lives that we cannot include in thanksgiving, the devil has found an open gate. What helpful consolation is available to the pastor is to make clear that "God has been gracious to you."

Second: here the problem is a hardening against those things that God has yet in store for us. The spiritually tempted person is trapped in the thought that it is too late, that the time of grace passed him by. The future has been stolen from God—even if it still belongs to God—and conceded to the devil, to whom it in no way belongs. Consolation here would be to make clear, "God has a future for each person which he will create through the Word. He still has great things in store for you. Now is your time of grace and salvation."

Third: with young Christians, the main cause of melancholy is hidden sin that remains unconfessed. One becomes anxious before God and still more before people. The hidden things must come to light. God helps only those who are ready to repent. Often the lacking readiness is to forgive another person. As long as I cannot wholly forgive the other, Christ is not my ruler but rather the devil is. Here the consolation is: "God claims you wholly and completely. Do *now* what God wants from you *now*."

Along with all this (1–3 above), what counts is that God was, will be, and is now gracious. This is the whole gospel for those who are beset with melancholy.

The person who is puzzled about faith means to take God seriously when he doubts that God is gracious toward him. But God is not taken seriously when one's own lostness is taken more seriously than the grace of God, which is able to take away and emerge victorious over that lost condition. It is also not taking God seriously when we elevate our concept of God as divine wrath above God's essence, namely the reality of God's grace. God is gracious above and beyond all our sins. Those who want to take God seriously should look upon Christ. In Christ God's wrath is revealed as nowhere else, yet at the same time

God's grace is revealed as nowhere else. If you think you are under God's wrath, then cleave to Christ! "For his anger is but for a moment, and his favor is for a lifetime" (Ps. 30:5).

Hidden and unknown temptations are the most dangerous. They are objectively present to us but subjectively we do not reckon them. Their aim is general ruin of our spiritual state. Signs of such temptations are that we can no longer pray, sense our sin, take refuge in grace and forgiveness, or have anything conclusive in which to believe. The whole Christian terminology is known and even respected; it rolls out of our mouths without a hitch, but it has no grip on our hearts. God's wrath is concealed in such circumstances. But the human heart is hardened to the point where one cannot recognize God's wrath even once. "To have no temptation is the worst temptation" (Luther).[36] Here our spiritual care must clarify where the foundation lies for such self-induced impenitence. This is one of the most difficult problems the pastor will face. He can only rely on the Word, which is sharper than any two-edged sword, and before which the thoughts and intentions of the human heart are laid bare (Heb. 4:12).

A brief word might be said in conclusion about those who are troubled by a lack of personal experience of God. To begin with, we should inquire about their thankfulness, hope, and obedience. Where these remain parenthetical and marginal to a person's being, grace will always be cheap grace. No doubt the best information is in remembering 2 Corinthians 12 where Paul asks for the removal of the "thorn in the flesh" and receives the answer, "my grace is sufficient for you." We have no claim to experiences of God. We will not be saved by experiences but by grace, not even through an *experience of grace* but by grace alone. Grace is more than what we "experience" of it. Grace has to be *believed*. Thus we mustn't gloss over sins. We would badly distort Paul's words if we did that. Sin is never a "thorn in the flesh" with whose presence we are to become content or comfortable. Sin must come to the light of day under all circumstances.

VI. SPIRITUAL CARE TO
THE SICK

Sick visits should be regular. Bear in mind that they are for the sake of the sick person. People never expect others to show up so much as they do when sick. It is best to schedule the visit in advance so the sick person can get presentable. Announced visits are more worthwhile than surprise visits. The pastor mustn't ignore a scheduled visit. You can't imagine how much damage you'll do if you don't show up. Scheduling regular visits pledges the pastor to be prepared and the sick person to be ready. If possible, the visits should always be scheduled at the same hour and on the same day of the week.

Regular visits are also good for the pastor. He should be present with the sick often. In such a way he will learn that sickness and health go together. This is not abnormal. Sickness and pain are a law of the fallen world. A person who happens to experience fallenness in this special way is an image of the One who bore our sickness and was so afflicted that people hid their faces from him (Isaiah 53). If Jesus came among the sick, that signifies that he bore the law of this world and fulfilled it. "He took our infirmities and bore our diseases" (Matt. 8:17). Jesus saves in that he bears. His salvation has nothing to do with magic, which is able to make people well from a distance. In Jesus' healings the cross is prefigured. Healing shows that Jesus receives and bears the sick in their weakness, a weakness he will bear on the cross. Only as the crucified One is he the healer.

Among the sick we learn more about the world and come closer to the pangs of Jesus' cross than we do among the well. Guilt, sin, and decay are more recognizable where everyone participates in the subjection of those who suffer without any particular discernible reason. The same curse rests upon us all. Some, however, experience it more deeply and painfully than all the rest. Such participation helps us recognize the true condition of the world. Our health is endangered in each moment. All sickness is enclosed within our health. The law of this world calls for a cross and not health. It's not good that the sick are shut up, concentrated in large hospitals to put them far out of sight of the well. At Bethel the sick and the healthy live with one another, sharing as a matter of course daily life and worship: a continual reminder to the sick of wholeness.[37]

Love toward sick members should have a special place in the Christian congregation. Christ comes near to us in the sick. The pastor who neglects the visitation of the sick must ask whether or not he can exercise his office on the whole.

Sick people ask for healing. They cry for release from this body of death into a new and healthy body. They cry for the new world in which "God will wipe away every tear, and there will be no more suffering or crying or pain" (Rev. 21:4). Insofar as this happens, the sick inquire about Christ more than do the well. Christ fulfills this conscious or unconscious expectation through his promise, "I am the Lord, your physician" (Exod. 15:26). Nevertheless the proclamation should not be limited to this one aspect. No proper spiritual care occurs without the offer of the forgiveness of sins. The mandate to proclaim the forgiveness of sins applies here, too. Often concrete sins will come to light. Not only past sins come to light, but also those related to the sickness and those the sickness itself creates. Sickness can make one egocentric and sullen, driven to extreme resistance toward Christ, a resistance which is itself unhealthy. The sickbed then becomes burdened with great guilt. So in spiritual care compassion cannot stand alone; we must also bring the whole truth of sin and grace.

To parishioners who are faithful at worship the pastor might bring the Sunday sermon. "I come because you are not able to come." He will tell the other, "You should know that the church is particularly attentive and pledged to the sick even when they are not able to attend church." Many people might wonder and silently suspect that someone wants something from them, perhaps is looking to use their condition toward some cheap end. It must be made clear to them that the church comes to the sick without ulterior motives simply to be with them and to help wherever help is desired. Through simple presence we show that God is with the sick and that sickness may be interpreted as a sign of God's nearness. The presence of the church and the offer of help are never more than pointers to that Help who is God.

There are disagreeable and selfish people. They offer no apologies; after all, they have been torn from their work, they cannot go home, and they fully expect the world to revolve around them. They need to see that their pretensions are groundless; they are, in fact, dependent on the love and friendship of others, and they only do more damage to themselves by such self-seeking behavior. They live in order to receive help. They should be thankful that this is so and learn to be patient when things don't go as fast as they would like. If they abjure thanksgiving and patience, then they destroy what blessing their illness may hold.

A special problem is presented by the big wards where people are crowded together. There is a lot of bickering in these wards, especially among old women. We might gently remind people that it is undignified to carry on so when we will all soon stand before the judgment seat of Christ. A conversational opening may be to ask how long the person has been ill and, above all, how his or her patience is holding out. One has to extend the right to the sick person to talk about how things are going. Just don't let the story become too long. Sick folks love to gab and they will go into as great detail as possible about their illness. Better information will be available from the patient's nurse.

Besides the pastor, doctors and nurses, and family gather at the sickbed. The pastor may, in confidence, limit himself to his own area of expertise. Above all, don't enter into technical medical conversations. Occasionally there may be a hidden struggle between doctor and pastor at the sickbed, most likely when the doctor thinks his care for the patient is all that is necessary. He would like to keep the pastor away with the argument that issues like sin, judgment, and eternity are beyond the daily necessities and shake up the patient too much. The pastor must not give up his mission in the least when this happens.

The sick person must not get the impression that, in his condition, he is unnecessary and useless. The pastor can give him such information and tasks that he will be able to see himself on the sickbed as if he were in the midst of the congregation. His chief task will be to intercede for the congregation as a whole and for specific needs, for the pastor and his ministry, for the life and struggle of the church, and also for the other sick people and for a good spirit of community. No one knows that as well as he does. He should know that this ministry, under the circumstances, is more important than all the hurried activities which well people are conducting outside the hospital. A by-product: prayer helps get people through sleepless nights. Those who pray won't have to worry that they will arise sleepy on the next day. Prayer will strengthen them.

It is also important to bring the sick something to read. Almost all sick people like to read, even things they would not pick up when well. They should be encouraged to name some biblical books or stories that can be kept on hand as introduction to further writings on the Scriptures. Tracts may be helpful. Written lectures are not a substitute for spiritual care but an aid and supplement to it. They may be referred to in a follow-up visit. All this will serve to control the quality of the available literature.

Truth belongs at the sickbed. The pastor should never come with cheap and false comfort that life will soon be all right once more. How is he to know that? On the other hand he shouldn't say that it will soon be all over. He has no certainty of that either. What the sick need to know in any event is that they are special and uniquely lodged in God's hand, and that God is the giver of life whether in this world or the next. Vision and heart must always be made opened up to that other world. "Be at peace and let your life rest quietly in God."

For spiritual care with the sick, it helps if the pastor knows as many Bible verses and hymn stanzas as possible by heart. The memorized Word is more effective and more easily implanted than our own. One might consider creating a booklet for the sick and dying with texts and songs.

Healing of the sick in the form of laying-on of hands must be briefly mentioned. That it should be made available goes without saying. No pastor should glory in it, however. Blumhardt always did it only in the presence of witnesses. With good reason; dangerous and exotic elements can creep into the practice all too easily.

Communion of the sick is not always advisable. In order to highlight the communal nature of the meal and to guard against magical conceptions of it, all the family members should participate.

VII. VISIT TO THE DEATHBED

If the pastor is called to a dying person's side, there is no reason by which he can excuse himself. Here we deal with people at the boundary of their existence and with a portion of their final decision. This is the last opportunity to speak a Word through which Christ can make his dwelling in that person; the last opportunity for conversion, confession, or absolution.

At the deathbed only proclamation of the gospel, confession, and absolution need transpire. One's final sighs ought to lead into the kingdom of God. Where forgiveness is not, there death reigns.

It should be possible for the pastor to have a moment alone with the dying person. He will ask if the person is distressed and would like to make a confession. Then he should ask if the person is wholly certain of salvation through Christ and takes comfort in it. This inquiry should end with absolution for all sins and assurance of the hope of life eternal.

Prayers for the dying should be kept short and spoken close to the ear. The young Blumhardt cried into his father's ear, "Father, the victory is won."

We should ask if the dying person understands that this is the end.

False respect for the dying is of no avail when salvation is at stake. It is not always easy to decide how much we should try to get a dying person to receive the Sacrament. It should never be forced on anyone. One can die in faith without the Sacrament. But in any event, the offer should be made.

The pastor will often experience the bitterness of death in its most horrible forms in his ministry. But the bitterness will be balanced by wonderful experiences at the deathbed. Often the moment of death is the moment of highest happiness and greatest joy. "God, is that beautiful!" Such experiences should lead one to thanksgiving and they will be an aid for our ministry with the sick and the dying.

> "I leave, as you have promised, Lord,
> in peace and gladness. . . . " (LBW 349)

VIII. CONFESSION AS THE HEART
OF SPIRITUAL CARE

The goal of all spiritual care is the confession that we are sinners. This confession actualizes itself preeminently in the confessional. So the confessional is the essential focus for all spiritual care. The invitation to confession is the invitation to become a Christian.

Confession is the common property of the Christian church. Confession has always stood in highest esteem in the Roman Church as well as in the Eastern church. Originally, the Reformation church held it in high esteem, too. Luther practiced it until his dying day. He protested that the Christian life could not be maintained without confession. In contradistinction from Roman practice, however, he moved away from compulsory confession and the necessary enumeration of all known sins. He intended us to move away from any pressure or torment connected with confession and to stress the value of its original meaning: confession is grace.

Luther distinguished three modes of confession:

a. daily confession to God in one's prayer;

b. public confession in the common liturgical confession of sins;

c. personal confession before a fellow Christian including a confession of concrete sins and a personally addressed absolution.

Luther contended that the first two modes of confession were obligatory; the third one was left up to the freedom of the Christian, but he urgently commended it as a divine offer which could make us sure of our salvation in Christ. "When I exhort people to confession, I am exhorting them to be Christians" (Large Catechism).

In his early period Luther recognized that any Christian had the right to hear a confession because of the universal priesthood of all believers; later he considered it to be more closely tied to the office of the pastor.

In the post-Reformation period confession became tied to the Eucharist and thus the exhortation to confession was always exclusively addressed to the faithful. After the recitation of the Creed came the absolution. In opposition to this alteration of confession into something doctrinally legalistic by the Orthodox, the Pietists moved confession into the context of the *collegium pietatis* or put it entirely into a private setting. As a result of this history, confession as an ecclesiastical institution was lost to us. Attempts to regain the practice for our own church (Loehe and Kliefoth in the nineteenth century)[38] met with negligible success. In our day the Berneuchen circle (cultic-institutional approach)[39] and the Oxford Group (using an approach outside the office of the pastor)[40] have tried, but on quite different grounds. Currently psychotherapy offers yet another approach from these two, as a secular offshoot of confession.

The foundations for confession and absolution are the gift and the mandate of Christ (Matt. 18:18–19; John 20:21–23; cf. also James 5:16; Eph. 4:25, 32; Ps. 32:1–5; Prov. 28:13). In our proclamation we must point out tirelessly what great grace God offers in confession and that people may not reject this offer with impunity. Only in such a way can confession win a place once more in the evangelical church. The following rules are intended to be helpful for preaching about confession.

If I go to confession I go to God. I am not confiding to a human being, rather this person stands wholly in God's stead. What I say to that person I say to God. He will guard it as God's secret.

The pastor is a called confessor. Thus the confession is not tied to personality. Confession belongs to the universal priesthood. Like the "mutual consolation among Christians" (Smalkald Articles) it is bound up with the faith of the Christian community.

The pastor cannot help us understand that our reluctance to use confession is groundless if he appears to live a life above and beyond daily trials. No one is beset with such difficult temptations as the Christian and especially the pastor. The devil is right there in his full being wherever the name of Christ is named. We do not understand sin through our experience of life or world, but rather through our knowledge of the cross of Christ. The most experienced observer of humanity knows less of the human heart than the Christian who lives at the foot of the cross of Christ. No psychology knows that people perish only through sin and are saved only through the cross of Christ. Anyone who has seen the meaning of the cross for but a moment is shocked by the godlessness of the world and by the awesomeness of his own sins; he will no longer be shocked by the sins of his sisters and brothers in Christ. The spirit of judgment is cut off at the roots. He knows the other to be accepted by God in the midst of his lostness even as he is accepted. He loves brother and sister under the cross.

Very little is understood of those to whom we are closely related—the son his father, the husband his wife, and vice versa. What happens here is that everything gets based on personal confidence and trust and the intimate address that results from trust. We seek to build an organ of understanding through our manner of speaking. But then we also place others in "roles" set off from ourselves. But a self-created role is never capable of containing a person. The true "role" is an office meted out by God, and bound up with the cross of Christ.

In confession everything depends on a personal absolution. In order for this to be certain I must call my sins by name. I come in order to receive. I can only do that when I have previously named my sins. Absolution does not require an expression of need so much as a confession of sin. I can distance myself from my need by unburdening myself on others, but absolution requires me to make a complete confession of sin. Confession is not only a self-expression, but a liberation from that which destroys my very life, not along the lines of a self-transformation but through the forgiving means God has given. These offer grace for the foundation, strengthening, and certainty of new life.

Why isn't confession of sin to God sufficient? Why must I confess to another human being? Here is a threefold answer:

a. Of course there is confession before God alone. Luther suggests that may be enough for the "strongest Christians." He reckoned himself, however, to be among the "weak," who need the assurance that God is not a phantom and that I do not simply forgive myself in the end. I receive this certainty through a fellow Christian. Without the presence of a flesh-and-blood confessor everything might be easily lost in pure reflection. It is quite treacherous if we find it easier to confess our sins before the Holy One than before a person who is no different from us.

b. All secret sins must come to light, if not now then at the last day. "For we must all appear before the judgment seat of Christ" (2 Cor. 5:10). Better now than later! As long as our sin remains hidden, it gnaws away at us and poisons us. Sin creates detritus in the soul. The serpent must stick its head out of its hole in order for it to be clubbed. When another person hears my sins their danger can finally be taken away.[41]

c. The root of all sin is pride. I want to live unto myself. I become a law unto myself. I may covet and I may also hate, for I alone am judge. In my pride I wish to be like God. Confession to another human being breaks this arrogance as nothing else can. The old, prideful Adam dies a disgraceful death in great agony. Since this humiliation is so painful, we would rather bypass it and think that it is enough to confess to God. But in our degradation we find our portion in the disgrace of Christ, who was not ashamed to stand before the world as a sinner. Confession of sin before another person is an act of discipleship to the cross. By confession we gain freedom from pride of flesh or reason.

Complete self-surrender to the grace, help, and judgment of God occurs in confession. Everything is surrendered to God; we retain nothing for ourselves. Thus we become free of ourselves. What separates us from obedience and from certainty—our thanklessness, our lack of readiness to forgive, the things we would cling to as uniquely our own domain—everything is surrendered to Christ and forgiven by him. In absolution God receives us once again in order to reign over our whole lives and to set us completely free. Confession is a conversion and a call to discipleship. We have nothing left, not even our sins; they are laid on Christ. He steps toward us and his joy and righteousness become our own.

Genuine community is not established before confession takes place. The whole community is contained in those two people who stand next to one another in confession. If anyone remains alone in his evil, he is completely alone despite camaraderie and friendship. If he has confessed, however, he will nevermore be alone. He is borne by Christ on whom he has laid his sin, and by the community which belongs to Christ and in which Christ is present with us. In the community of Christ no one needs to be alone.

Confession is grace, not law. It is not a work we do in order to become perfect Christians; it is a grace which leads to certitude, conversion, fellowship, and joy. Confession is divine sadness which leads to divine joy. Confession as a pious work is the devil's invention and leads to spiritual death. Where people lament that there is no life in the church we might ask how that is connected to disregard for confession. In any event, new life in Christ, new obedience and service, and new joy in the gospel all stem from confession.

Only those who make confession should hear confessions. In a monastery the abbot must confess to a brother before he hears confessions. Only those who have been humbled in the confessional are able to hear confessions without pride. Otherwise it is too easy to turn a ministry based on the love of Christ into a form of domination over the souls of others.

The confessor must learn to say candidly, "I am the chief of sinners. My sin is inexcusable." He walks with Christ in his daily rounds. He owes others a friendly admonition toward confession. He will keep those who come to confession in his intercessions. He will help to the end that confession is not seen as a once-for-all matter, but as that which accompanies another on the way. He will render confession its rightful objectivity.

Course of events: announcement. Appointment of a set time. Quiet in and around the confessional room. Prayer. Silence. Opportunity for confession. Keep any pastoral conversation short. Absolution (in either the form of a prayer or a declaration). Concluding prayer of thanksgiving.

Excursus: Help for spiritual care in connection with confession. In the evangelical church, exercises are taboo. They raise the inevitable suspicion of works-righteousness. It is too easy to overlook the fact that they are only a *means* to help and not help itself. Help only comes in the form of God's forgiveness and renewal. There is only one preparation by which we reach out to God's means, one openness and readiness to receive God's gifts in our lives. That is thanksgiving and obedience as response to God's grace and by which we know that grace has won a substantial place in our lives. Exercises for the one who gives spiritual care are made concrete in such things as Bible reading, meditation, prayer, abstinence, silence, and humble service to the neighbor. In the background stands the old dogmatic relationship between contrition of the heart, confession with the lips, and satisfaction by works. We must regain the New Testament and evangelical sense of this threesome. We should not try to bypass the necessity of such exercises.

a. Exercises prior to confession. It's probably best to begin with one of the commandments. But no impossible things should be required. To one who has had a falling-out with his parents the pastor might say that he should finally quit his self-righteous behavior. He might counsel an adulterer to go away so that he won't see the woman with whom he was destroying his marriage for a long time. He might request the proud person to be cordial once more to those with whom he has not been friendly.

The pastor should always be concerned with giving easily fulfillable requirements. The goal of any such exercises is to replace the "I can't." When it becomes clear to a person that "I can't" means "I won't," spiritual care gains accordingly. It helps to remind people that these requested exercises are not a commandment but a counsel. The counsels have their legitimate theological locus in this context.

b. Exercises after confession. The situation is simple when injuries perpetrated on others come to light in the confessional. They must be put right. If there is no intention to do that, then the confession cannot be authorized. But apart from such clear situations, certain exercises become necessary because of our inconstancy. New doubt may usher itself into our lives. The prospect is dangerous, threatening tomorrow and the day after tomorrow. The flesh with its renewed demands must be conquered and disciplined. That can happen when we humbly serve the neighbor. Bible reading, meditation, prayer, and suggested denials have their place, too. In all these exercises following confession the aim is to preserve the grace that has been received and to live from it. They are an ongoing element in the Christian life. To those who find them repugnant they appear as a hard law. To those who are willing, however, they are a gentle yoke in which our wild cravings find a rest.

IX. SPIRITUAL CARE FOR PASTORS

Preface: The relationship between pastors is decisive for the church. Nothing is more destructive for a congregation than personal animosity or outright hatred. Through such things the pastor will heap guilt on himself. The rule should be never to say anything against one's co-pastor, in any event nothing adversely critical. An older pastor is invari-ably given more honor than a younger one or one who was called to the congregation at a later date. It would be foolish to forget that the con-gregation is always enamored by a new pastoral face. One should never give assent to any gossip or scandal against the other pastor.

It is amazing how frivolous pastors can be out of sheer vanity. When visiting in homes one must be constantly aware of this, otherwise you can besmirch your office. A special problem in this regard is posed by the first visits of a new pastor. Those who are not the best parishioners may try to burden us with gossip or complaining out of a sense of com-plaisance or simply out of stupidity. We must be on guard to preserve the solidarity of the office.

If the church is the body of Christ, then its servants are indissolubly bound to one another. The other pastor is not merely a colleague in the calling, but a brother or sister. One lives in commonality with those who receive and serve the body of Christ. This commonality helps us, indeed it bears us. That is a result of common service and stems from the essence of the church.

Mutual help in ministry is taken for granted. But we need more; we need another to care for our soul. Everyone who cares for the soul needs a person who will care for his or her soul. Only one who has been under spiritual care is able to exercise spiritual care. That law is part of the very essence of the church. Those who renounce that law will have to face the consequences in their work. We need someone to intercede for us daily. Those who live without spiritual care move easily toward magic and domination over others. One finds oneself thus unable to be faithful anymore. One preaches, administers the sacraments, carries out the obligations of the office—but is faithless. Thus the office becomes a curse.

Not everything should be introduced into spiritual care. Spiritual care cannot absorb the entire realm of human or Christian experience. There are things one should be prepared to come to grips with on one's own. When one is no longer able to do this, then spiritual care should be sought. If *everything* is made subject to spiritual care, we may wind up with a lack of self-understanding. The goal of spiritual care is rather to lead people along in their own struggle to the point where they can break through it on their own. Excessive dependence on spiritual care can result in lack of resistance and inner laxity. One's own experience thus never matures, and we abandon the attempts too soon.

Intercessory prayers by the pastor on behalf of the congregation ought to include all fellow pastors. Let the pastor be attentive to the request for intercession. To promise intercession and then not do it is very bad. The most helpful prayers are those about which the other is unaware.

The pastor should intentionally seek spiritual care about the responsibilities of the office. Whoever takes the office seriously must cry out under the burden. One has to make visits, listen to and bear the needs and sorrows of many people; one has to carry on numerous conversations with those one accompanies on life's way and always with those who encroach on one's time. One should make intercession for not a few people and, in order to do that properly, has to stay informed. One has to find the right word with the dying, at the graveside, for a wedding. One should—and here is the heaviest responsibility of all—preach out of genuine certitude in order that others are led to certitude. One should read and meditate upon Scripture. Where can a pastor find rest and recollection for all this work? We have to recognize that there are mortal dangers for the office and for those who exercise it. Even the responsible, serious, and faithful pastor may be driven to external or internal perplexity. This can be a pure lack of faith. In the end, perplexity leads to insensitivity. The load is too heavy to bear alone. We need someone who will help us use our powers in ministry correctly, someone who will defend us against our own lack of faith. The activist and the resigned, lazy pastor are flip sides of the same coin and are equally dispensable: both of them lack silent, ordered prayer and spiritual care. If the pastor has no one to offer him spiritual care, then he will have to seek someone out. Only through prayer will mission and skill come together in an orderly relationship. The mission is huge and our skills are small. The two are united in prayer. In prayer I experience the mission anew but not so that it overcomes me; rather it is wrapped in assurances of divine power and joy. We do not receive such divine aid all at once, but the pastor must beg for it daily—the saying remains true: "God gives us a burden, but God also helps us bear it" (Ps. 68:20 in the Luther Bible).

The greatest difficulty for the pastor stems from his theology. He knows all there is to be known about sin and forgiveness. He knows what the faith is and he talks about it so much that he winds up no longer living in faith but in thinking *about* faith. He even knows that his nonfaith is the right form of faith: "Lord, I believe; help my unbelief" (Mark 9:24). Knowledge reveals his daimonism. It drives him further and further into factual unbelief. We can then have no experience of faith. Our only experience is reflection on the faith.

The problem is exacerbated by our constant preaching. We have to say things we have not experientially discovered. Such "misuse" of the Word must bother us very deeply. Indeed it is our singular mission not to preach our experience but to preach from Scripture. That can be proven and justified on the best theological grounds. Everything indeed depends on the Word. But it's a sorry state of affairs if we are not bothered that our experience lags so far behind the Word, or if we strike the pose of a martyr who, renouncing his own experience, subjected himself for the sake of proclaiming a strange Word. The peak of theological craftiness is to conceal necessary and wholesome unrest under such self-justification. In this case, one cannot believe because one doesn't want to believe. The conscience has been put to sleep. Theology becomes a science by which one learns to excuse everything and justify everything. This justification even has ultimate authority from Luther, from the Confessions, and finally from the New Testament. The theologian knows that he cannot be shot out of the saddle by other theologians. Everything his theology admits is justified. This is the curse of theology. One cannot express this without anxiety and embarrassment. *It must be the theology.* But here it is worth repeating: "Whoever loses his life for my sake will find it" (Matt. 16:25).

Whoever has once begun to justify himself with the help of theology is in the clutches of Satan. Naturally Satan is a great theologian! But he keeps your understanding three steps removed from your body. Otherwise it might be threatening for your life: you might fall into a swamp where your faith will suffocate. When one appears so hollow, there is no way to convince him theologically that experience can never be decisive and that faith depends on an objective base. The only help is to call a person to the simplest things of Scripture, prayer, confession, and to concrete obedience in one definite matter. And to allow himself to be led forward step by step by Christ.

The life of the pastor completes itself in reading, meditation, prayer, and struggle. The means is the word of Scripture with which everything begins and to which everything returns. We read Scripture in order that our hearts may be moved. It will lead us into prayer for the church, for brothers and sisters in the faith, for our work, and for our own soul. Prayer leads us into the world in which we must keep the faith. Where Scripture, prayer, and keeping the faith exist, temptation will always find its way in. Temptation is the sign that our hearing, prayer, and faith have touched down in reality. There is no escape from temptation except by giving ourselves to renewed reading and meditation. So the circle is complete. We will not often be permitted to see the fruits of our labors; but through the joy of community with brothers and sisters who offer us spiritual care, we become certain of the proclamation and the ministry.

X. THE FUNERAL

The intent of Christian burial is not to eulogize the deceased, nor is it a farewell to the deceased. Christian burial has, from the beginning, differed consciously and significantly from that of the heathen. Christian burial is a recollection of the hope which is given our body, not only to the soul. The body is to be raised up, *Somatikos*. Christian burial is illuminated through joy over the resurrection of Christ and fully expects the manifestation of his victory over our death. At the same time it is a recollection of the burial of Jesus. The body is laid to rest even as the body of Jesus was brought to its rest. We become like him in this and thus participate in the promise which lay over his body imbedded in the earth. The Christ who was laid to rest is the same Christ who was raised up. Thus we signify in burial the identity of the buried body with the body of future resurrection and eternal life. For this reason the body is honored with all deference.

What does participation by the congregation signify? And in what does it consist? The congregation is the body of Christ. All within it belong together as members of a single body. When one dies, it is as if a member of the body has been separated. But this member is also simultaneously received by the lord of the body, Christ. He ushers the person along on the pathway to fulfillment. The death of a Christian is thus more than the passing away of a person in solidarity with the vanishing of all other creatures. The day of burial always bears the stamp of a hidden joy for the congregation. In the hour of death the prayer-bell rings. This ringing calls the congregation spiritually into the last hour. The Christian cannot be alone. Christ and the saints are with him, to suffer and die with him. Who dies, with him the whole community dies (Luther). On the Sunday after the death the congregation makes intercession on behalf of the dead. Can intercession for the dead be generally maintained as correct in the evangelical church? The Reformed answer this question in the negative. Yet Luther considered such petitions to be possible: "One should pray for the dead two or three times and then stop."[42] Given this limitation, intercession serves as a substitute for prayer at the hour of death in which the whole congregation could not participate. This becomes the final act of participation in the life of the deceased and not—as the Roman Church teaches—the first act in a new relationship that must then be permanently repeated. These limited intercessions consider the life, hope, and faith of this particular person to be really finished and uplifted definitively to the mercy of God. Those petitions for the dead that are stretched out over a long period of time show lack of contentment with the mercy of God. This is faithlessness. We should and may believe God's mercy for these dead persons and not continue to question everything. Through death, God himself established a boundary for all those activities that bring a person to faith and salvation. God's decision (predestination) and human decisions converge at death. No dogmatic assertion about the descent of Christ into hell can be made into an objection to taking death seriously as boundary for all decisions about salvation or its loss. The descent is an attempt to answer the question whether the generation before Christ must remain excluded from salvation. Such an attempt does not brook any systemization. Blurring the boundary between life and death will always end in a depreciation of life and of the call to salvation which is made to us here and now. Where the human heart supposes that intercessions and masses for the dead can alter the decision, this knowledge must act as a preventative. For the dead, everything depends on God alone who has declared his support. The heart must love God above all things, knowing that with God all things will reach a fitting conclusion. So in any case that final, limited intercession for the dead must understand this: "The Lord preserve thy coming in and thy going out."

In conclusion, participation by the congregation at the funeral shows that the community knows itself to be in an indestructible fellowship, through Christ, with the one who has fallen asleep in the Lord. For those who die in faith the last judgment has already taken place and they are already brought from death to life (John 5:24).

The service of mourning at home. Where this is still customary it makes good sense. The community is making one final visit to the home of the deceased. This is a witness to the deceased (and the family) that he lived in a Christian home. This helps the family's separation from the one who has died. Christ comes in the guise of the congregation to the home and, in return, the house comes to Christ again, that is, at the funeral. The family's claim on the dead is dissolved by the right of the body of Christ. The one who has died has become wholly a member of the community. The congregation receives him from the family and brings him to the place where the community sleeps and awaits the coming of Christ.

The cemetery. The cemetery is the place where *the* community that sleeps and waits is gathered. Since one is bound up with others in this life, one will also here be awakened together with others. The relative right to establish denominational cemeteries stems from this fact. The congregation beautifies this place, because here the bodies of the saints wait. It is a special piece of earth intended for the seed which is planted in it and for the hope of resurrection.

The cemetery surrounds the church to show that the place of worship is simultaneously the place of burial. The whole congregation is gathered here, the church militant and triumphant, those who are still being tested and those whose trials are over. With this in mind, it makes good sense to inter within the church where it is possible.

The pastor should visit the cemetery as often as he is able. This is wholesome for him personally, for his preaching, for his spiritual care, and also for his theology!

The question of cremation. Prejudice against cremation has endured through early, medieval, and modern times. Overall, wherever Christianity came in earlier times, the tradition of cremation was broken. In the Middle Ages the heretics, who were believed to be excluded from salvation and from the resurrection, were burned and their ashes scattered to the four winds. The reintroduction of cremation in modern times was, at least in its earliest stages, a conscious affront to the Christian hope of resurrection. All the other viewpoints—hygiene, economics, the lack of cemetery space in large cities—have come to the forefront with the passage of time. This history has made it difficult for the church to come to a positive judgment about cremation in an intelligent manner.

There are no final dogmatic reasons against cremation. The strongest argument against it may be the image of the buried Christ. The Christian might prefer to be laid to rest as was his Lord. The body which is bound up in such a great hope with God may command such respect that one prefers not to hasten its destruction. These matters may be left to personal preference. It is a relative matter whether one advises interment or cremation. But in no way should one refuse to participate in a rite of cremation.

Interment as a congregational matter. The community called church is one on earth and in heaven. The congregation on earth lives, through its Lord, in the most intimate relationship with the heavenly congregation. Those who have died are in reality those who live and those living on earth are the dying. The cemetery is the place of life's victory. Here lie those who live with the Lord.

The homily should express our thanks to God the Creator for the earthly life which has come to an end. A few specific things from the person's life might be brought to our attention. Otherwise there is an easy pattern to follow. One should give thanks for the faith of the departed, that God gifted him with Word and Sacrament and ministry in the congregation, for his witness in vocation and family, for his public church attendance, for his preservation in sickness and death. With such lives God paves the way for praise and thanksgiving in the world.[43]

We should not silence the scriptural truth that death is both the wages of sin and also the end of God's wrath. Still less should we be silent in our witness to Christ who has conquered death. "With peace and joy I enter in . . ." is appropriate. Our sorrow is overcome through faith and hope; we need to keep in mind, however, that too speedy a reconciliation with death might be a bit enthusiastic and incomplete.

We should deal restrainedly and gently with the question about seeing one's loved one again in the kingdom of the resurrection. We lose each other for a brief time in order that we might have each other back in eternity (Philemon 15—16). The less interest put on this question and the more exclusively we focus our hope on Christ, the more we are able to discuss things dispassionately. The question has its origin as a consequence of bodily resurrection and the preservation of our identity. We were created for one another, and this "for one another" includes a mutual discernment. Discernment belongs to the essential marks of the congregation (1 Cor. 13:12): "Now I know in part; then I shall understand fully, even as I have been fully understood."

Baptized non-Christians and non-Christian mourners. This situation is quite different than the case of interment of a Christian with congregational participation. The sermon should deal, as in the case of a Christian, with thanks for the friendliness God displayed toward the person. In order to avoid the risk of idle talk, one should mention specific things where possible. Just don't talk about what you don't know! You devalue everything else you have to say and make yourself incredible. One should not be silent about indifference to Christian faith or opposition and hatred toward the faith. Thus the pastor, at the interment of Hofmann von Fallersleben, said, after the recital of many positive things, "Yet this man was a fool because he did not recognize the presence of Christ in his life." Such a judgment, naturally, can proceed only from a firm knowledge of the deceased and only after continual and earnest pastoral efforts with him. Interment is more than a proclamation to the congregation. It is an activity having to do with the dead. Truth must override all other considerations, especially false respect.

Particular care must be taken with the proclamation of comfort. One should not extend comfort where it is not desired. One should not describe the pain of the mourners. People take simple pleasure in solitary grief. Grief is one of the secular forms of immortality: " . . . as long as there is grief the dead live on." As false comfort, it is a flight from discomfort. The truly concerned and healthy person wants no one who offers comfort to understand comfort as a substitute for that which is his responsibility. In the midst of his perplexity over such a boundless loss he knows that there is no comfort available on earth, no one able to give comfort. The pastor must express this knowledge, too. The pastor may not give a moment's notice to false expectations. The way to genuine comfort does not proceed by degrees from false reasons for comfort; it can only be heard if the false reasons are driven out. Comfort consists in that Christ has been raised from the dead and through him God has become our God and is the One who makes all things new. None other can step into this emptiness. The gap shall and must remain until God alone fills it, the Giver stepping into the place of the gift, the perplexed winning joy through the will of God who remains forever. The pastor can be a poor mourner and comforter at the same time. He should not try to enter into the mourners' grief all that much. All individual pain is uplifted in his mission. The pastor should use a text prophetically for the hearers, and perhaps he might, with the family, look for the confirmation text of the deceased. Then the text will have an entirely different effect on the hearers than if he came unprepared.

If another person speaks, a philosophical or political speaker, that should happen only after the funeral liturgy is over. The pastor should make clear that he takes no responsibility for the content of such speeches. If possible he should ask another speaker to share, in advance, what he intends to say.

The funeral of a suicide. Only in cases where some form of church discipline was being exercised is any refusal or alteration of the funeral warranted (for example, without tolling the bells or wearing vestments). Why should a suicide be treated any differently from those who die unrepentant? At the interment speech one should not gloss over the manner of death, but one should also not moralize or condemn. It is our fault if a Christian brother takes his own life. It is much too late for church discipline at the graveside. It should have been exercised earlier in an attempt to stop the member from taking his life.

The meal after the funeral. This can be a healthy and helpful practice. After the deceased has been laid to rest a great sense of desolation can overcome the mourners. One doesn't know how to get started with life again. The depressing atmosphere needs some relief. The pastor may offer a prayer of invocation. In the churches of rural Pomerania it is customary to sing spiritual songs at this time. That is a commendable idea wherever it is possible. Among Christians a joyful tone is permissible if it is quiet. The pastor should pay attention to a fitting conclusion to this time of being together.

It is necessary to visit the house of the deceased twice. The first time is prior to the funeral and then at a later time. The second visit is expressly for spiritual care.

XI. THE WEDDING

The marriage contract is a secular matter. The marriage license is issued by the registrar's office. Here the matter is concluded before God and humanity. The church's wedding is related to the state service through the proclamation of the Word, the announcement of a blessing, and the intercessions on behalf of the marriage. In the registrar's office the marriage receives its public recognition. A private marriage can be a genuine marriage. But it receives neither the protection nor the publicity of the state. Without this public recognition the marriage may become burdened and the wife especially may feel uneasy.

Marriage is a "secular matter" (Luther) but not political. It is not contracted *through* the registrar but *before* him as an official of the state by the man and the woman. The Nazi State considers marriage to be a political organization. Arranged marriages are forbidden and the children of such marriages are liable to seizure. That is a clear transgression of the state's competence. The boundaries of political order are hard to fix. It is only possible through a system of checks and balances. The parental order of preservation is in no way political, but in fact stands over against such an ordinance." The fourth commandment is not political. Luther speaks against such an understanding when, in his explanation to the fourth commandment, he extends the honor and obedience due parents to "authority." The political ordinance is not worthy of faith; it is wholly secular. The order of marriage and parenthood, however, has its own right before God and limits the right of the state.

Conversation with the bridal party. It serves a purpose to go through the order for marriage. Here there are three things to highlight: marriage as divine institution and life in marriage as life in an "estate"; the cross of marriage; the promise and blessing of marriage.

The bridal couple should be advised that they come already to the marriage service as a married couple. Let nothing false be said!

The wedding homily. The homily may begin with thanksgiving to God the Creator. God speaks even to the creation out of pure grace. Every creature is invited to take delight in its good creator. God has directed our longings in a wonderful way to this place. Though we always turn away from the will of God and oppose it because of our human desire, God accepts that desire and blesses it in marriage. This is a great mystery.

It is God's ordinance which is consummated here. Marriage is a divine estate, protected by the Word of God. The sixth commandment was given to uphold the worth of marriage and hold it sacred.

God is Lord over marriage. He will never abandon his ordinance.

Under the lordship of God marriage has an internal order so that the man functions as lord only by loving his wife, while the wife is subject to her husband likewise in her love for him. It should be clearly stated how that looks and what it means.

On such a marriage the beneficence and blessing of God rests. As a visible sign of blessing God may give children to the marriage. Children are not our work to dispose of, but rather a gift of God.

How can one conduct a marriage in accordance with God's commandment? Only through faith in Jesus, since he is the source of forgiveness, love of neighbor, chastity, and obedience. One must also proclaim the Second Article at weddings.

Therefore the marriage should be subjected to the Word of God and to the One who would like to make this marriage a part of the body of Christ right now. The calling of marriage is to be the body of Christ.

The congregation is entreated to intercede on behalf of this marriage.

XII. BAPTISM

Preparation. It is essential to hold a pastoral conversation with the parents prior to the baptism. Both parents should take part in the baptism, otherwise the baptism should not be authorized. A sponsor's letter should be given to the godparent. Agreement with the contents of this sponsor's letter should be the condition for their acceptance as godparents.[45]

The baptism should only take place in church, preferably in the context of the Sunday worship service.

Suggestions for a baptismal homily. Thanksgiving for the gift of the child.

Connected with this is the note that the child is only entrusted by God to the parents.

The relationship between natural birth and spiritual regeneration, flesh and spirit, death and resurrection, sin and forgiveness. A possible preaching text: "that which is born of flesh . . . " (John 3:6).[46]

The child is saved out of the world in the community of the church. One should not speak of an invisible church, but of the one that is present here and now.

At baptism only the fixed formulas of vows should be used.[47]

Works Cited

The following works were referred to by Bonhoeffer in the lectures.

George Bernanos. *Die Sonne Satans.*
———. *Tagebuch eines Landpfarres* (ET: *Diary of a Country Priest*).
C. Buchsel. *Erinnerungen aus dem Leben eines Langeistlichen.*
P. Geyser. *Besuch an Sterbebetten.*
Thomas à Kempis. *Imitatio Christi* (ET: *The Imitation of Christ*).
Luther's Sermone aus dem Jahr 1519.
J. Arndt. *Anweisung zum seligen Leben.*
Chr. Blumhardt. *Von Reich Gottes.*
———. *Vom Glauben bis ans Ende.*
J. Gotthelf. *Geld und Geist.*
F. Timmermanns. *Der Bauernpsalm.*
F. Dostojewskij. *Schuld und Suhne* (ET: *Crime and Punishment*).
———. *Die Bruder Karamasow* (ET: *Brothers Karamazov*).
———. *Der Idiot* (ET: *The Idiot*).
A. Fr. Chr. Vilmar. *Gewalt uber die Geister.*
H. Asmussen. *Seelsorge.*
das Gesangbuch, especially the hymns of Paul Gerhardt.[48]

Notes to Spiritual Care

1. Hans Asmussen was born in 1898 and was active in the church in Denmark and northern Germany. He was associated with the Berneuchen movement, a liturgical renewal group in the German Church, and wrote a number of books. In 1934 Chr. Kaiser Verlag of Munich published his *Die Seelsorge*. While the topics covered are the same as those Bonhoeffer covers, Asmussen's third chapter is entitled *"Seelenfeuhrung,"* which we translate as "spiritual direction" (pp. 43–79). Asmussen sets up a dialectic between this and *Seelsorge*; the former is the means by which we educate people living in the here-and-now; it lies between the extremes of the *gemeinschaftliche* and the *landeskirchliche* and its task is to dispel the illusion that we can live on an island of faith separate from daily and national concerns. *Seelenfuehrung* thus enables people to live in human community and create a public meaning based on their faith; it is grounded in First Article theology, for if we confess the creation we must create meaning in the world we see and experience. Asmussen suggests that if we lose First Article theology, not much will come of the Second and Third Articles.

More importantly, Asmussen says that *Seelenfuehrung* is specifically connected with the law *(Gesetz)* and *Seelsorge* with the gospel *(Evangelium)*. For Asmussen the proclamation of the law as part of spiritual direction rests on a concept of the "godfearing person" and also upon the notion of crisis theology that one must be brought to a moment of decision. Spiritual direction is for those who are not yet able to reach certitude in matters of the faith. Bonhoeffer, as the text shows, disagrees about the separation of law and gospel into two approaches to pastoral care; he brings both law and gospel into the one format of *Seelsorge*.

2. Perhaps a reference to Mark 1:21–34; cf. also chap. 22 in Dietrich Bonhoeffer, *The Cost of Discipleship*, trans. Reginald H. Fuller (New York: Macmillan Co., 1960), 183–84.

3. See Dietrich Bonhoeffer, "Breaking Through to Community," in *Life Together*, trans. John Doberstein (New York: Harper & Bros., 1954), 112.

4. This note was, of course, made into a clarion call in *Cost of Discipleship*; it forms the basis for the whole book and is specifically mentioned at the beginning, chap. 1, p. 35.

5. The concepts of *Amt* and *Stand* have deep rootage in Lutheran theology

back to the confessional writings of the sixteenth century. There we learn that the "call" is central to the bestowal of the *Amt*. No one may preach or teach *"ohne ordentlichen Beruf"* (*"nisi rite vocatus"*: Latin) according to the Augsburg Confession, and this call is at the center of the evangelical understanding of ministerial office (*Amt*). Through God's commandment life is organized and channeled through these "offices and estates" (*Staende*). Bonhoeffer began to reorganize his thought in this area in the 1930s when, in 1932, he spoke of orders of preservation in the brief work, "Thy Kingdom Come" (in John Godsey, *Preface to Bonhoeffer* [Philadelphia: Fortress Press, 1965], 27–47). In *Ethics*, he spoke at length of the *Mandaten* (mandates) of preservation whereas the German Christians were in defense of the orders of creation-concept.

"'For lack of a better word,' Bonhoeffer chooses the term 'mandate,' for 'institution' or 'order' is too easily associated with 'a divine sanction for all existing orders and institutions in general and a romantic conservatism,' while the term 'estate' is too suggestive of 'human prerogatives and privileges.' As for the concept of 'office,' finally, it has been 'so completely secularized' and is too closely 'associated with institutional bureaucratic thinking.' All these negative connotations are to be excluded and overcome by the concept of 'mandate,' which at the same time is only of a 'temporary' nature and finally served 'to renew and to restore the old notion of the institution, the estate, and the office'" (Timo R. Peters, "Orders and Interventions," in *A Bonhoeffer Legacy: Essays in Understanding*, ed. E. J. Klassen (Grand Rapids: Wm. B. Eerdmans, 1981), 314–29, cit. 321.

6. One suspects Bonhoeffer has more in mind than the sermon in his term *Predigt*; in concert with his later material on the place of law and gospel, one supposes he means the whole notion of the Word of God as taught in the theology of the Word by Barth and Brunner.

7. Probably another reference to Asmussen, who uses these terms in his text.

8. Bonhoeffer later personalized this in the sections entitled "Proving," "Doing," and "Love" in *Ethics*, trans. R. Gregor Smith, ed. Eberhard Bethge (New York: Macmillan Co., 1955), 161–76, which speak of the discernment of God's will which begins in our recognition that we don't know God's will, a recognition to be made daily, out of which comes renewed decision-making power and responsibility. *Seelsorge* uses the familiar form of the *Seelsorger* to bring us to this point of recognition.

9. Cf. *Cost of Discipleship*, 60–66, for a lengthy discussion of the text.

10. Cf. chap. 3, "Single-Minded Obedience," in *Cost of Discipleship*, 69ff.

11. "This is a happy discovery for the Christian who begins to pray for others. There is no dislike, no personal tension, no estrangement that cannot be overcome by intercession as far as our side of it is concerned. Intercessory prayer is the purifying bath into which the individual and fellowship must enter every day. The struggle we undergo with our brother in intercession may be a hard one, but that struggle has the promise that will gain its goal," *Life Together*, 86.

12. Cf. "The Ministry of Listening," in *Life Together*, 97–99, esp. 98: *Seelsorge* "is essentially distinguished from preaching by the fact that, added to the task of speaking the Word, there is the obligation of listening."

13. More is at stake here than meets the eye. In the lectures on preaching delivered during the same period as part of the curriculum at Finkenwalde, Bonhoeffer says:

> "Conversion can have results just like political propaganda. There have been conversions to Hitler that are exactly analogous to some 'conversions' to Christ. This phenomenon can occur in the preaching of Christian evangelists. In the case of such conversions a falling away inevitably follows. The person 'converted' was swept off his feet and later all he feels is embarrassment. Then it is doubly difficult to bring him back to a healthy religious position. An apparent conversion is a dangerous menace for Christians. It is not simple to distinguish between 'psyche' and 'pneuma.' Generally speaking, both have their place. But where we see raw psychology at work we must oppose it" (*Worldly Preaching*, ed. Clyde E. Fant [Nashville and New York: Thomas Nelson, Inc., 1975], 163–64).

14. One wonders how Bonhoeffer would have reassessed this stance at a later date. His prison persona is relaxed and no barriers of *Amt* exist; cf. Martin Marty, *The Place of Bonhoeffer* (New York: Association Press, 1962), 13, about Bonhoeffer divesting himself of "clerical mannerisms."

15. Bonhoeffer's attitude toward psychoanalysis has been long marked as polemical and inimical; he calls psychotherapy, as he knew it, a "secular asceticism" (the original translation in *Ethics* said "secular Methodism," but we follow Godsey's suggestion (from his essay on translation in *Bonhoeffer in a World Come of Age*, ed. Peter Vorkink II [Philadelphia: Fortress Press, 1968]) which seems less tendentious.

James Woelfel, in his *Bonhoeffer's Theology*, draws attention to Bonhoeffer's reserve and reticence, going so far as to suggest these qualities were, for Bonhoeffer, a mark of Christian maturity. There are several indications of that reserve in *Seelsorge*, particularly where Bonhoeffer discusses visitations in the home and the pastor's own life. Clifford Green's comment deserves full quotation:

> "By temperament and family training Dietrich Bonhoeffer was reserved about just those areas of the human psyche which psychoanalysis was probing. Respect for reticence was deeply imbedded in his character. Inquisitive prying into people's inner life was repugnant to him, as was promiscuous self-disclosure. Uncovering everything that exists was not, he felt, truthfulness but cynicism. He was averse to 'talking openly about sexual matters,' and after reading a 'remarkably frank' French novel about marriage, he wrote that 'the naturalistic, psychological novel is no longer adequate'; he was also very wary of narcissistic people who took themselves too seriously. As his poem 'Who am I?' shows,

Bonhoeffer was something of a psychological agnostic" ("Two Bonhoeffers on Psychoanalysis," in *Bonhoeffer Legacy*, 58–75, cit. 63–64).

Green points out further that an interview with Dr. Paul Jossman, an associate of Dr. Karl Bonhoeffer, disclosed that Dietrich did not inherit his condemnatory attitude from his father: "Jossman insisted that he could not have adopted this attitude from his father" (ibid., 65).

Bonhoeffer lumps "psychotherapy" and "existential philosophy" as a single structure worthy of dismissal, but in fact does not make any distinctions between forms of psychotherapy or forms of existential philosophy. His own beloved Kierkegaard seems not to be included in the list of existentialists, and many have pointed out that his thought would be welcomed by Camus. The rejection of psychotherapy is surely influenced by his early interest in Barth, perhaps especially in Barth's *The Word of God and the Word of Man*, which came out in 1928 and which Bonhoeffer read prior to the seminar he took with Barth.

Green is again helpful when he notes that Bonhoeffer's theology in the *Letters* (*Letters and Papers from Prison*, enlarged edition, ed. Eberhard Bethge [New York: Macmillan Co., 1972]) includes aspects of anthropology which would be shared by psychology as marks of maturity, for example, independence, autonomy, responsibility, and acceptance of reality (Freud). The emphasis on the weakness of God is also significant, if subtle: "Seen from a psychological perspective, the 'weak' Christ removes at a stroke the powerful God wished for by weak egos. The cosmic screen on which the religious person projects fantasies of compensatory power is chopped down. In its place stand the cross and the Christ who frees religious people from infantile dependence, sending them back to find God in their strengths, knowledge, responsibility, and happiness" (ibid., 70).

Thomas Oden argues that Bonhoeffer tried to overcome the jurisdictional dispute between therapy and theology in a number of different ways. He suggests that since for Bonhoeffer "the reality of God discloses itself only by setting me entirely in the reality of the world and when I encounter the reality of the world it is always already sustained, accepted, and reconciled in the reality of God" (*Ethics*, 61), there may be an "unconscious faith" operant in therapeutic process, with grace fully present and at work.

This solution to the problem is rooted in the concepts of *fides directa* and *fides reflexa:* the latter is the conscious response of a person to the Word of God as known in Christ. The former may be operant within the worldly processes, which are emancipated to be what they are and in which we receive the invitation to true worldliness. Thus therapy lives in "relative autonomy," allowed to function within its own format in accordance to its own innate and developed processes, but in the last sense not interpretable only from within its own limited framework.

"The great limitation of a spuriously autonomous psychotherapy is not that it fails to elicit any healing or authenticity, but that it would define authenticity only from within the narrow range of the client's own self-understanding, instead of his being understood by God" (Thomas C. Oden, "Theology and Therapy: A New Look at Bonhoeffer," *Dialog* 5 [Spring 1966]: 98–111; cit. 104.

16. An "Introduction to Daily Meditation" was prepared by Eberhard Bethge under Bonhoeffer's supervision for inclusion with the Finkenwalde circular letter of 23 March 1936. It is found in Dietrich Bonhoeffer, *The Way to Freedom*, ed. E. H. Robertson, trans. E. H. Robertson and John Bowden (New York and Evanston: Harper & Row, 1966), 57–61. The problems of daily meditation were well known to the Finkenwalders; some rebelled against the discipline in the early months (see *I Knew Dietrich Bonhoeffer*, trans. Kaethe Gregor Smith, ed. Wolf-Dieter Zimmerman and R. Gregor Smith [New York and Evanston: Harper & Row, 1966]).

17. Cf. "Intercession," in *Life Together*, 85–87, for expanded notes.

18. Cf. *Life Together*, 113, about "meeting the congregation in one brother."

19. Cf. the essay "The First Table of the Ten Commandments," in *Preface to Bonhoeffer*, 49–67. Here Bonhoeffer clearly points out that we are not concerned with an abstract law but with the Giver of life; not with recognizable laws of life but with God's "I"; not with a Lord but with *the* Lord (esp. 50–53). Bonhoeffer wants us to know that the Ten Words remain Word, that is, they are not detachable as something called "God's Will," but are always address, a living Word from the living God.

20. Later, in *Ethics* (1943), Bonhoeffer expressed clearly what is becoming obvious here; "commandment" does not mean only the condemning function of the law, but is rather to be seen as Torah, as the foundation of the world: "the commandment of God is something different from what we have so far referred to as the ethical. It embraces the whole of life. It is not only unconditional; it is total. It does not only forbid and command; it also permits" (244).

21. In Whitsuntide, 1937, Bonhoeffer invited local pastors of the Pomeranian Church to Finkenwalde and presented a paper on church discipline, "The Power of the Keys and Church Discipline in the New Testament" (*Gesammelte Schriften*, 3:369ff.); this was a difficult problem in light of the collapsing of the Confessing church structure; Bonhoeffer argued that the matter belonged to the congregation as an aspect of the gospel.

22. Cf. the section "Adam" in Bonhoeffer, *Temptation*, trans. Kathleen Downham (London: SCM Press, 1955), 14–16.

23. Bonhoeffer was of the view that absolution should not be granted following a general confession, but that the absolution was in the Holy Communion. Bonhoeffer's comment: "the expression of grace should be no absolution. The forgiveness of sins takes place through the preached Word and the receiving of the Sacraments" (*Worldly Preaching*, 151). This is connected to Bonhoeffer's view that repentance has no individual aim but leads to community; cf., for example, "The Nature of the Church," in *The Way to Freedom*, 47.

24. See, for example, *Cost of Discipleship*, 50–60, where Bonhoeffer comments on the passage, Luke 9:57–62.

25. Some discipline is envisioned in the pastor's life similar to that which per-

tained in the seminary community at Finkenwalde, which began with prayer and meditation on Scripture in the morning; see chap. 2, *Life Together*, 40–75. See also chap. 1 of *The Way to Freedom* to help put the notes on spiritual care in the context of this unusual preachers' seminary. See also, Eberhard Bethge, *Dietrich Bonhoeffer, Man of Vision, Man of Courage* (New York and Evanston: Harper & Row, 1970), chap. 9, 341ff., on "Preachers' Seminary."

26. In this connection one might see the section in Gabriel Marcel, *Creative Fidelity*, 27–28, where Marcel notes that Americans do not have the same deep sense of "at-home-ness" one finds among Europeans.

27. Bonhoeffer's use of scripture is seen in the writings *Psalms* (trans. James H. Burtness [Minneapolis: Augsburg Publishing House, 1970]), *Temptation, Creation and Fall* (trans. John C. Fletcher [London: SCM Press, 1959]), *Cost of Discipleship*, "The Interpretation of the New Testament" (308–25 in *No Rusty Swords*, trans. John Bowden, ed. and intr. Edwin H. Robertson [New York and Evanston: Harper & Row, 1965]), his sermons and the essay "King David" in GS IV, 294–320; Godsey's *Preface to Bonhoeffer* is a translation of two studies, "Thy Kingdom Come," and "The First Table of the Ten Commandments." Notes throughout *Letters and Papers from Prison*.

Further studies include John Godsey, *The Theology of Dietrich Bonhoeffer* (Philadelphia: Westminster Press, 1960), 119–94; Walter J. Harrelson, "Bonhoeffer and the Bible," in *The Place of Bonhoeffer*, 115–40; Geffrey B. Kelly, "Freedom and Discipline: Rhythms in a Christocentric Spirituality," in *Worldly Preaching*, 130–52; see also pertinent sections in Dietrich Ritschl, *A Theology of Proclamation* (Richmond: John Knox Press, 1960).

Gerhard Ebeling's chapter, "The Non-Religious Interpretation of Biblical Concepts," in *Word and Faith*, trans. James W. Leicht (Philadelphia: Fortress Press, 1963), 98–161, attempts to grapple with Bonhoeffer's approach to scripture with only partial success since there is a discrepancy between his and Bonhoeffer's concept of *Gesetz*.

Two essays in *A Bonhoeffer Legacy* relate to this: Douglas C. Bowman's "Bonhoeffer and the Possibility of Judaizing Christianity," 76–88; and James W. Woelfel, "Biblical Agnosticism and the Critique of Religiosity," 281–93. On the relation of Bonhoeffer to the so-called Old Testament, see Martin Kuske, *The Old Testament as the Book of Christ* (Philadelphia: Westminster Press, 1976).

What is certain about Bonhoeffer's approach is that he immersed himself in Scripture through devotional reading (cf. *Letters and Papers from Prison*), that his preaching was rooted in contemplation of the Word (Fant, *Worldly Preaching*), that he was not principally an exegete (Harrelson), and that his understanding of the place of the Old Testament shifted over the years to the point where he could say, in *Letters and Papers from Prison*, "he who desires to think and feel in terms of the New Testament too quickly and too directly is in my opinion no Christian" (trans. in *Interpretation*, vol. XII [July 1958]). Lastly, it is clear that Bonhoeffer strongly believed that one lived as a nonreligious Christian only by immersion in the text as concrete historical reality that deals with the practicalities of life and not with "spiritual" or "eternal" verities; cf. John A.

Phillips, *Christ for Us in the Theology of Dietrich Bonhoeffer* (New York: Harper & Row, 1967), 84–94, on Bonhoeffer's interpretation of the Christocentric, theological, and devotional interpretation of Scripture: "From the very beginning of his interest in the problem of scriptural interpretation, he was intensely involved with the question of *how one related oneself to scripture; how scripture became actual and concrete in life*" (89).

28. In "Thy Kingdom Come," Bonhoeffer identifies the three powers that enslave the earth through the one power of the evil one as death, loneliness, and desire, which cannot be overcome in a utopia but solely through the *Gemeinde (Preface to Bonhoeffer*, 35).

29. The educated *(Gebildete)* come under heavy criticism in the writings of Bonhoeffer, perhaps because he was well acquainted with the problem, since he came from this well-educated class. The sketch, "After Ten Years," which referred to the ten years of Nazi rule, contains a section which speaks of the loss of ground under everyone's feet *(I Loved This People*, trans. Keith R. Crim [Richmond: John Knox Press, 1965], 18). In the novel fragment, Christoph (who is Dietrich) testifies eloquently to the dissolution of life he has experienced in a society that has rendered the old goals impossible by its nihilism: " . . . but what happens if there are already forces at work which render impossible, intentionally, any living and getting along together? What if a struggle has already been proclaimed to us in which there is no communication, only victory or defeat?" *(Fiction from Prison*, trans. Ursula Hoffmann, ed. Renate and Eberhard Bethge with Clifford Green [Philadelphia: Fortress Press, 1981], 124). See also David Hopper, *A Dissent on Bonhoeffer* (Philadelphia: Westminster Press, 1975), 107.

30. A good description is in "Thy Kingdom Come," 37.

31. *The Cost of Discipleship* may be read in its entirety as a critique against Culture-Protestantism.

32. Cf. "The Ministry of Helpfulness," in *Life Together*, 99–100.

33. *Acedia* is the opposite of joy: "Since ancient times, accidie—sorrowfulness of the heart, 'resignation'—has been one of the deadly sins. 'Serve the Lord with gladness' (Ps. 100:2) summons us to the Scriptures. This is what our life has been given us for, what it has been preserved for up till now. Joy belongs, not only to those who have been called home, but also to the living, and no one shall take it from us" *(True Patriotism*, ed. E. H. Robertson, trans. E. H. Robertson and John Bowden [New York and Evanston: Harper & Row, 1973], 189).

Hilarity is the mark of the joyous person; weakness and strength also figure into this dialectic (cf. Hopper, *Dissent*, 99–133); the weak are to be borne by the strong, whose lives are characterized by *hilaritas*, which is "confidence in (one's) own work, boldness and defiance of the world and of popular opinion, a steadfast certainty . . . " *(Letters and Papers from Prison*, 229).

34. The seven deadly sins are pride, lust, anger, avarice, envy, gluttony, and sloth *(acedia).*

35. Bonhoeffer uses this term in its meaning as given by Heidegger; this is

the only occurrence of it in the notes on spiritual care, and it appears deliberate. *Dasein* is "the mode of being peculiar to the one who is, distinct from other forms of being"; see *Act and Being*, trans. Bernard Noble (New York and Evanston: Harper & Row, 1961), 20. *Dasein* is God's being God, not merely God's existence *in se*. *Acedia* robs us of the certainty of that particular presence. (Cf. also *No Rusty Swords*, 55–57, for a critique of Heidegger.)

36. A note already sounded by Bonhoeffer in *Temptation*, 44: "no temptation is more terrible than to be without temptation."

37. Bethel bei Bielefeld is a famous center for healing and care in Germany which was developed under the leadership of Friedrich von Bodelschwingh (6 March 1831–2 April 1910) and others, including Bodelschwingh the younger, beginning in 1872. It is one of the most remarkable institutions to derive from the Inner Mission movement: it was also the locus of the first confession of the Confessing Church; cf. Guy Carter, "Confession at Bethel, 31 August 1933: Forgotten Witness?" An essay presented to the Annual Meeting of the International Bonhoeffer Society for Archive and Research—English Language Section (1984). On the Inner Mission movement, see Jeremiah Ohl, *The Inner Mission* (Philadelphia: United Lutheran Publication House, 1911).

38. Both were leaders of the confessional revival in Germany in the nineteenth century. Wilhelm Loehe (2 February 1801–2 January 1872), the better known of the two in our time, was a leader in the deaconess movement and in missions; he spent his entire ministry in the small town of Neuendettelsau, Bavaria. His writings are best known in *Three Books Concerning the Church*, trans., ed., and intr., James L. Schaaf (Philadelphia: Fortress Press, 1969). Loehe's teaching on spiritual care is masterfully covered in Kenneth Korby, "A Theology of Pastoral Care in Wilhelm Loehe with Special Attention to the Function of the Liturgy," Th.D. diss., Concordia Seminary-in-Exile, 1976.

39. The Berneuchen Circle began in 1923 as a movement for liturgical reform; in 1931 the Circle formed the *Michaelisbrudershaft* (St. Michael Society), a wider group, to carry on conversation and scholarship. Out of the "spiritual week" it developed, which was devoted to Scripture, communion, song and prayer, many new orders for the chief service, confession, and daily offices grew. Leaders of the movement were Karl Bernhard Ritter, Walter Lotz, H. D. Wendland, and Bishop Wilhelm Staehlin. They sought to find a theological rootage for liturgy and revival that would encompass all of the German Church. Bonhoeffer was in communication with this group (the father of his fiancée of later years was closely connected with it), but withheld any commitment to it; he was, in fact, critical to the end of any liturgical renewal that smacked of antiquarianism or bogged down in minutiae (cf. *Letters and Papers from Prison*, 148, and the essay by Fuller in *Cost of Discipleship*, 169–94).

Bonhoeffer's criticism of the Berneuchners is summed up in a short statement in *Letters and Papers from Prison*, 328, where he says, "Those who, like for example Schuetz or the Oxford Group or the Berneuchners, miss the 'movement' and the 'life,' are dangerous reactionaries; they are reactionary because they go right back behind the approach of the theology of revelation and seek for 'religious' renewal. They simply haven't understood the problem at all yet, and their talk is entirely beside the point." Bethge notes (*Bonhoeffer, Man of Vision*, 360–61), "From the point of view of church politics, most liturgiologists, particularly those of the Berneuchen movement, displayed indifference toward church politics, so that they were suspect of the Confessing Church and often subject to judgments that are over-harsh. 'Only he who shouts for the Jews can sing the Gregorian chant,' Bonhoeffer once remarked to his ordinands in this connection."

40. The Oxford Group, from 1938 known as Moral Rearmament, was associated with the name of a Lutheran pastor from Pennsylvania, Dr. Frank Buchman (1878–1961); the movement began when Buchman lectured at Oxford University in the mid-1920s; emphasis was placed upon personal change with the catch-phrase "world-changing through life-changing," which Bonhoeffer found distasteful because he thought it shifted the gospel emphasis from forgiveness to the person's own belief and behavior (cf. Bethge, *Bonhoeffer, Man of Vision*, 388–89). The movement was further embroiled in controversy because of Buchman's strident anti-Communism and his voiced admiration of Adolf Hitler (cf. his speeches in *Remaking the Word* [New York: R. M. McBride, 1949]; and Peter Howard, *Frank Buchman's Secret* [Garden City, N.Y.: Doubleday & Co., 1961]).

41. "Sin demands to have a man by himself. It withdraws him from the community. The more isolated a person is, the more destructive will be the power of sin over him, and the more deeply he becomes involved in it, the more disastrous is his isolation" (*Life Together*, 112; on first part of paragraph, see *Cost of Discipleship*, 261).

42. This somewhat unusual quote comes from the witness of Apo. XXIV (The Mass), paras. 94–96 (Tapper, 267); Luther offered a form in his sermon *von dem reichen Mann und dem armen Lazarus* (22 June 1522): "Oh my god, this soul is in your hands and power, do with it according to your divine will and pleasure." The exact quote in our text is found on p. 369 of Luther's "Confession Concerning Christ's Supper," 161–372 in vol. 37 of the American edition (trans. Robert Harley Fischer). Masses for the dead are forbidden in the above writings, but not prayers. In the post-Reformation period, the church orders of Wittenberg and Baden (1556), Schwaebisch-Hall (1615), and Lutzelstein (1605), among others, made provision for such prayers after the sermon in the mass.

43. A further comment on death is to be found in the circular letter of 15 August 1941: "In the face of death we cannot say in a fatalistic way, 'It is God's will'; we must add the opposite: 'It is not God's will.' Death shows that the world is not what it should be, but that it needs redemption. Christ alone overcomes death. Here, 'it is God's will' and 'it is not God's will' come to the most acute paradox and balance each other out. God agrees to be involved in something that is not his will, and from now on death must serve God despite itself

. . . . Only in the cross and resurrection of Jesus Christ has death come under God's power, must serve the purposes of God. Not a fatalistic surrender, but living faith in Jesus Christ, who died and has risen again for us, can seriously make an end to death for us" (*True Patriotism*, 124–25).

44. In *Ethics*, in the final notes, Bonhoeffer works with a renewed understanding of the ways in which we are called by God in the world. He shifts the terminology from *Amt* and *Stand*, commonly called in English the "orders of creation," to the notion of mandates of preservation (*Mandaten*, 254–67). By so doing he indicates that God orders human life through commandment (*Mitzvah*; in German, *Gebot*); for Bonhoeffer, the *Gebot* is a vehicle of grace. The contrasting terms in classic Lutheran theology are *Gesetz* and *Evangelium*, the *Gesetz* (law) being that aspect of God's revelation which judges and condemns humanity. Bonhoeffer's understanding of the *Gebot* is closer to Judaism's understanding of Mitzvah as the positive, open-ended, invitational means to live one's existence before God in the world.

There are four mandates of preservation for Bonhoeffer: church, marriage and family, culture, and national government. Earlier (*Ethics*, 208) he also included work. He chose these terms for several reasons: first, because *Amt* and *Stand* conveyed a sense of human power which relieved the mandate of its dignity and humility before God; second, because the misreading of the orders allowed the political powers to usurp the function of God; the notion of "order" seems, from one point of view, to root the order in the very being of God where it is unalterable and where it seems to be before/behind Christ, and Bonhoeffer was also interested in change and growth in the mandates. The flaw in the "orders of creation" is the failure to reckon human sinfulness, which then allows the "orders" to be sanctioned solely as part of creation (cf. Woelfel, *Bonhoeffer's Theology*, 239–42).

45. In a treatise on baptism from 1942, Bonhoeffer argues that the faith of godparents is important because they are the witnesses on behalf of the child, but in any event they witness only because faith is come to us in Christ; the tasks of godparents are intercession and instruction within the community, based on faith and hope in the promises of Christ for the child (*True Patriotism*, 154–56); see also *Letters and Papers from Prison*, which shows Bonhoeffer's pride at being a godparent (195, 304) and his notes on their duties (309).

46. In *Cost of Discipleship*, 205–11, Bonhoeffer states that the major occurrence in baptism is the death of the old self and the arising of the new (esp. 207); in the treatise of 1942, he says, "baptism is the translation of a man into the eschatological community, incorporation into the Body of Christ, which really takes place through a physical action ordained by Christ. In it there takes place the washing away of sins, being born again, dying and rising with Christ, receiving of the Holy Spirit, being made one with the image of Christ, and being sealed in the eschatological community for the day of judgment. All this happens without any cooperation and activity on the part of men, as Christ's own action (Eph. 5:26) in his community (*True Patriotism*, 148).

47. Bonhoeffer is here most likely thinking of the period known as rationalism, during which many private agendas for worship were written in which the baptismal formula was changed into a nondescript assertion of the presence of a vague god in the child's life, usually leading to morally upright behavior and often associated with the privilege of culture and education. An example is from the "Evangelical Church Agenda for Preachers who are not expressly bound to a Regional Liturgy" (i.e., *Kirchenordnung*, one of the many regional orders for ministry and worship in the German Lutheran Church):

"I therefore baptize thee, dear N. N. to the glory of God the Father, of his Son Jesus Christ, and of the Holy Spirit"

which is followed by numerous descriptions of the meaning of water in common and ritual use. This agenda, by no means the worst of the lot, was written by one J. F. Schlez in 1834.

48. Bonhoeffer's love of hymnody is well known and documented throughout the Bethge biography; one may also consult the letters in *Letters and Papers from Prison* for numerous references; *Life Together*, 57–61, relates to the use of hymnody in the community (Bonhoeffer is harsh on polyphonic singing, preferring unison so that there are no prima donnas vying for attention). Paul Gerhardt (1607–1676) was Bonhoeffer's favorite hymnographer. His hymns cover the spectrum of the church year, which may be the reason for their popularity with Bonhoeffer, whose devotional life was rooted in the seasons of the year. Hymns of Gerhardt currently in the American *Lutheran Book of Worship* are nos. 23, 46, 105, 116, 129, 276, 336, 454, and 465; these include hymns for Advent, Christmas, Lent, Holy Week, Easter, Evening, and general hymns of trust in God. Among his best known hymns are "Oh Sacred Head, now wounded" (*LBW* 116); "Now Rest Beneath Night's Shadow" (*LBW* 282); and "If God Himself Be For Me" (*LBW* 465).

Bibliography

A. WORKS BY BONHOEFFER
IN ENGLISH

Act and Being. Trans. Bernard Noble, introduction by Ernest Wolf. New York and Evanston: Harper & Row, 1961.

Christ the Center (a new translation). Trans. Edwin H. Robertson, New York and Evanston: Harper & Row, 1978.

The Communion of Saints. Trans. R. Gregor Smith. New York and Evanston: Harper & Row, 1963.

The Cost of Discipleship. Trans. Reginald H. Fuller. New York: The Macmillan Co., 1960 reprint of 1949 first edition.

Creation and Fall. Trans. John C. Fletcher. London: SCM Press, 1959.

Ethics. Trans. R. Gregor Smith, ed. Eberhard Bethge. New York: Macmillan Co., 1955.

Fiction from Prison. Trans. Ursula Hoffman, ed. Renate and Eberhard Bethge with Clifford Green (in the English edition). Philadelphia: Fortress Press, 1981.

I Loved This People. Trans. Keith R. Crim, intr. Hans Rothfels. Richmond: John Knox Press, 1965.

Letters and Papers from Prison, enlarged edition. Edited by Eberhard Bethge. New York: Macmillan Co., 1972.

Life Together. Trans. with intr. John Doberstein. New York: Harper & Brothers, 1954.

Prayers from Prison. Interpreted by Johann Christoph Hampe. Philadelphia: Fortress Press, 1978.

Preface to Bonhoeffer, being two essays, "Thy Kingdom Come" and "The First Table of The Ten Commandments." Trans. with comments by John Godsey, Philadelphia: Fortress Press, 1965.

Psalms: Prayer Book of the Bible. Trans. James H. Burtness, with sketch of Bonhoeffer's life by Eberhard Bethge. Minneapolis: Augsburg Publishing House, 1970.

No Rusty Swords. Trans. John Bowden, ed. and intr. Edwin H. Robertson. New York and Evanston: Harper & Row, 1965.

Temptation. Trans. Kathleen Downham. London: SCM Press, 1955.

True Patriotism. Trans. E. H. Robertson and John Bowden, ed. and intr. Edwin H. Robertson. New York and Evanston: Harper & Row, 1966.

The Way to Freedom. Trans. E. H. Robertson and John Bowden, ed. and intr. Edwin H. Robertson. New York and Evanston: Harper & Row, 1966.

Worldly Preaching, by Clyde E. Fant; contains the lectures on preaching (pp. 123–180). Nashville and New York: Thomas Nelson, Inc., 1975.

B. SELECTED WORKS
ABOUT BONHOEFFER

J. Martin Bailey and Douglas Gilbert, *The Steps of Bonhoeffer: A Pictorial Album,* with foreword by W. A. Visser 't Hooft. New York: Macmillan Co., 1971.

Eberhard Bethge. *Costly Grace: An Illustrated Introduction to Dietrich Bonhoeffer.* Trans. Rosaleen Ockenden. New York: Harper & Row, 1979.

———. *Dietrich Bonhoeffer, Man of Vision, Man of Courage.* New York and Evanston: Harper & Row, 1979 (the biography).

———. *Prayer and Righteous Action in the Life of Dietrich Bonhoeffer.* Ottawa: Christian Journals Ltd., 1979.

———. "The Challenge of Dietrich Bonhoeffer's Life and Theology," The Alden-Tuthill Lectures, *Chicago Theological Seminary Register,* Vol. LI, No. 2 (February 1961).

Thomas I. Day. *Dietrich Bonhoeffer on Christian Community and Common Sense.* New York and Toronto: Edwin Mellen Press, 1982.

Otto Dudzus, ed. *Bonhoeffer Brevier.* Munich: Chr. Kaiser Verlag, 1979 (a compendium of brief readings for each day of the year from the Bonhoeffer corpus, in German).

Andre Dumas. *Dietrich Bonhoeffer: Theologian of Reality.* Trans. Robert McAfee Brown. New York: Macmillan Co., 1971.

Theodore A. Gill. *Memo for A Movie: A Short Life of Dietrich Bonhoeffer.* New York: Macmillan Co., 1971.

John Godsey. *The Theology of Dietrich Bonhoeffer.* Philadelphia: Westminster Press, 1960.

Clifford Green. *Bonhoeffer: The Sociality of Christ and Humanity.* Missoula, Mont.: Scholars Press, 1972.

David H. Hopper. *Dissent on Bonhoeffer.* Philadelphia: Westminster Press, 1975.

Geffrey B. Kelly. *Liberating Faith.* Minneapolis: Augsburg Publishing House, 1984.

E. J. Klassen, ed. *A Bonhoeffer Legacy: Essays in Understanding.* Grand Rapids: Wm. B. Eerdmans, 1981.

William Kuhns. *In Pursuit of Dietrich Bonhoeffer.* Foreword by Eberhard Bethge. Garden City, N.Y.: Doubleday Image Books, 1969.

Martin E. Marty, ed. *The Place of Bonhoeffer*. New York: Association Press, 1962.

Heinrich Ott. *Reality and Faith: The Theological Legacy of Dietrich Bonhoeffer*. Philadelphia: Fortress Press, 1972.

John A. Phillips. *Christ for Us in the Theology of Dietrich Bonhoeffer*. New York: Harper & Row, 1967.

Larry Rasmussen. *Dietrich Bonhoeffer: Reality and Resistance*. Nashville: Abingdon Press, 1972.

James Woelfel. *Bonhoeffer's Theology: Classical and Revolutionary*. Nashville: Abingdon Press, 1970.

Wolf-Dieter Zimmerman and R. Gregor Smith, eds. *I Knew Dietrich Bonhoeffer*. Trans. Kaethe Gregor Smith. New York and Evanston: Harper and Row, 1966.

Glossary of Common Terms _____

Bonhoeffer uses a consistent vocabulary in his works and the following German words have been consistently translated into English by a particular word.

Amt *Office*

Anfechtung *Temptation* and, where the sense in which Luther used *Anfechtung* is clearly indicated, *spiritual trial.*

Beichte(n) *Confessional, make a confession,* in the sense of the sacramental and ritual forms of repentance done before a pastor.

Bekenntnis *Confession,* in the sense of a confession of faith; usually refers to the history confessions of the Reformation Churches, the Barmen Declaration, etc.

Gemeinde *Congregation* and/or *community.* The word means more than congregation in most instances; it has the meaning Bonhoeffer intended for "community" in *Spiritual Care.*

Gemeindeglied(er) *Parishioner*

Gemeinschaft *Community*

Predigt *Sermon.* Though the word has a broader meaning than our usual sense of the word "sermon," there is no good alternative, since it must be compared with *Verkuendigung* (see below).

Seelsorge *Spiritual care,* translated this way to avoid the confusion of the term "pastoral care," which has overtones in the contemporary arena of psychological counseling not intended by Bonhoeffer.

Seelsorger *Curate of souls,* where that is applicable, and sometimes just *pastor.*

seelsorgerlich *Pastoral*

seelsorgerliches Gespraech *Pastoral conversation*

tragen *To bear.* This word is very important to Bonhoeffer in many of his writings; the double entendre in the English usage of the word is the same in German.

Verkuendigung *Proclamation,* always meant as the law and the gospel (*Gesetz und Evangelium*) as a unity. Not the same shade of meaning as *Predigt* (above).